P9-AFW-607

Copyright © 1991 by John Wiley & Sons, Inc.

All rights reserved. Published simultaneously in Canada.

INTRODUCTION AUX METHODES PRATIQUES DU SERVICE edited by École Technique Hôtelière TSUJI was first published in Japan by Kamakura Shobo Publishing Co., Ltd. © 1988 École Technique Hôtelière TSUJI.

Library of Congress Cataloging-in-Publication Data
Professional restaurant service / École Technique Hôtelière Tsuji.
     p.   cm.
   Includes bibliographical references.
   ISBN 0-471-53828-0 (cloth)
   1. Food service.   I. École Technique Hôtelière Tsuji.
   TX943.P717 1991
   642.6–dc20   90-24651

Printed and bound in Japan
10 9 8 7 6 5 4 3 2 1

Preface

When we envision a dining scene, we must encompass the full scope of those involved. This scene is composed of, and may be divided into, three distinct arenas. The first two may be plainly apparent to you: (1) those who partake in the preparation of the meal and (2) those who dine. However, the third arena—those whose responsibility it is to make the meal a pleasurable experience—is rarely noticed.

The realization of a truly gratifying dinner is dependent on many variables. First, it is dependent on the diner's health and overall mood on that particular day. Furthermore, it may depend not only on the chef's culinary techniques but also on suitably selected ingredients and the zeal with which they are prepared. However, I firmly believe that the most important element is the work of the individuals who shape all of this into a satisfying meal—that is, the service staff.

This service is a pivotal point of a wonderful dinner. Granted, an onlooker may simply perceive it as somehow graceful and congenial. But it is much more than that. The greatest possible care is taken by the service staff in the performance of their jobs, and there is a great deal of knowledge and experience required to carry out their work.

The service staff should, first of all, invariably be neat and particular concerning their personal appearance. They should speak clearly and crisply. They should move easily and gracefully and they must be able to smoothly dominate the proceedings in the dining room and kitchen, without any obvious behavior. They are important but should be self-effacing—I am inclined to compare them with air. Their actions and behavior in the dining room are critical in creating the ambience essential for a superior dining experience.

The service staff must be capable of quickly recognizing guests' intentions: do they prefer to finish eating quickly, do they wish to remain longer to savor the meal, or is the meal only secondary to the business being discussed? The service staff must know how to behave in any of these situations. At times they must keep their distance from guests in order not to disturb them, but they must remain attentive to their every need. It is truly a back-breaking job. Service staff must also possess a swift and precise memory and be capable of concealing their emotions, regardless of the situation. Working in the dining room may indeed require a special disposition in addition to a set of learned techniques.

In Japan, culinary techniques have come to rank with those in Europe. I established Tsuji Hotel School as an academy for the young man and woman seeking to achieve the same level of excellence in the sphere of restaurant service.

Within this book, you will find a compilation of the basic service techniques employed in a restaurant of the highest standards. It is my wish that this book will provide a thorough grounding in service and enable many to become superior service practitioners.

Shizuo TSUJI
President,
École Technique Hôtelière Tsuji

Contents

Wine Service

French–English Glossary

1

A Short History of Restaurant Service

The Origin of the Restaurant in France

In the Middle Ages people ate and drank at inns called *auberges*, which were beginning to be built along the roads, at public houses called *tavernes*, and at cabarets in the towns. At first, *tavernes* were allowed to serve nothing but drinks. Later they were allowed to serve foods such as appetizers (which they bought from delicatessens outside, like a charcuterie or rôtisserie), but they were forbidden to employ chefs in order to serve prepared dishes. Under the influence of *cabarets*, however, which were allowed to serve meals, *tavernes*, too, gradually came to serve substantial meals, and the differences between them disappeared.

In the middle of the eighteenth century a Parisian tavernkeeper named Boulanger decided to sell a dish of sheep's feet, or trotters, in a white sauce in his eating house. The advertisement for the dish read: "Walk up, everybody who has a weak stomach. I'll restore you." The French word for "restore" is *restaurer*. This nourishing dish gradually became associated with the word *restorante*, meaning "restorative food," and eventually the place where it was eaten came to be called a *restaurant*.

However, the restaurant as we know it was born in the late eighteenth century. The first one was the *Grande Taverne de Londres*, opened by Antoine Beauvilliers. It fulfilled all the conditions for a first-class restaurant as defined by Brillat-Savarin. That is, it provided every luxury imaginable—choice wines, attractive dinnerware, tidy waiters, and faultless, smooth service. As these fine restaurants evolved and prospered, service has developed to a fine art.

Changes in Forms of Service

Originally the French word *service* referred to the dishes served; later it came to mean the method of serving. The earliest forms of service were French service, which was used until the mid-1800s, and Russian service, which replaced the French and is the present form of service (see Figures 1 and 2 on pages 12 and 13).

French service was a luxurious form of service that originated at the courts and palaces of nobles. Even at a palace of a great noble, however, it was used only on special occasions. According to this type of service, a meal consisted of three courses. The first course included soups, *relevé* (a large roast of meat or a whole fish), the *entrée* (several kinds of dishes), and various *hors d'oeuvres*. The second course included roasted meat or chicken, salad, and *entremets*. (Initially, there were two types of *entre-mets*—light vegetables or garnishes and sweets. Now, *entremets* means side dishes, specifically sweet dishes served between courses or as a dessert. The last course included various kinds of desserts and fruit. For each course, the dishes were not served individually; instead, they were placed on the table all at one time.

Often with French service the beauty and abundance of the dishes became more important than their taste. For example, when serving many dishes at one time hot dishes were likely to get cold, but constantly warming these dishes compromised their quality.

Early in the 1800s, the Russian ambassador to France, Kourakine, noticed the faults with French service and decided to introduce another method. He believed that guests would better appreciate the taste of the dishes if each dish were served individually—hot dishes served while hot, and cold ones served while cold—as was done in Russia. However, this method could not take the place of the popular French service method; in fact, it took nearly 50 years for Russian service to become an accepted method. Urbain Dubois, a chef who worked under a Russian duke, enumerated the merits and demerits of both Russian service and French service in his introduction to *La Cuisine Classique* (1856). He stated that Russian service was more reasonable because guests were served as much food as they wanted and could taste dishes at their best in terms of quality. Throughout the nineteenth century, this form of service was introduced at an increasing number of restaurants and grew tremendously in popularity. Of course, there was still a tendency to consider it better to serve as many dishes as possible. However, the introduction of Russian service represented a turning point in the history of service. More attention gradually came to be paid to the method of serving, and the Russian service method continued to develop.

According to the method of service used today, if a guest finishes a dish, the used plates are removed immediately and replaced with fresh, clean plates. Wine glasses are placed on the table on the guest's right side, and wine is served from the guest's right as well. The waiter first pours a little wine into the host's glass, and the host samples it. When it has been approved, the waiter continues serving the wine to the other guests. Or, at an informal dinner, the host carves the food for the guests himself, and the plates with the carved meat are passed to the right of the host. Compared with French service, this is a much simpler method.

In the Middle Ages, *entremets* meant various entertainments between meals (*entre-mets*). Gradually these spectacles were replaced by light vegetable or sweet dishes served between courses, and, as meals decreased in quantity, the vegetable *entremets* were assimilated as garnishes and the sweets became desserts.

From the end of the nineteenth century to the beginning of the twentieth century, the expansion of the railway and the introduction of the automobile provided

FIGURE I

French style service. The French service style of earlier times included the use of a large ornamental stand called a *surtout*, which sat in the center of the table and about which dishes were placed symmetrically. Very often, tall gold and silver ornaments, fruits, candies, or flowers were placed on the *surtout*.

Figure 1

for remarkable development in the system of distribution and resulted in a rapid increase in the pace of life. The elaborate cuisine that required much time and labor to prepare could not keep up with the change. The cuisine that was started by Carême and had been gradually increasing its ornateness was destined to disappear.

Auguste Escoffier explained that culinary art, "for its expression, depends on the psychological state of mind of the society. The two are inseparable and thus the impulses from one are directly reflected in the other. ...As the pace of society increased, so did the requirements of the customer" (*Le Guide Culinaire.*). Escoffier presented a form of cuisine to meet the needs of the times. The cuisine became simpler. Dishes became less ornamental by using several sorts of vegetables as garnishes on each plate. Separate courses were introduced, establishing the menu we now know—the first course is hors d'oeuvres; the second is soup, followed by a light fish dish and a heavier meat dish; and the last course is dessert. These menu changes also prompted changes in the form of Russian service. The

13

FIGURE 2
Russian style service. The old Russian style of service comes closest to our setting now. The table was prepared with a set of cutlery and glasses for each guest. The *surtout*, with figurines on it, was positioned in the center of the table and circled with very ornamental dishes and a big sugar-work decoration. (Figures reprinted from *La Cuisine Classique* by Urbain Dubois and Emile Bernard.)

Figure 2

three standard forms of service in common use today are French service, Russian service, and American service.

1. **French service.** This form is often used in haute cuisine restaurants, since it tends to produce an elegant and gracious atmosphere. The food is attractively arranged on platters and presented to the guests, after which the preparation of the food is completed on a table beside the guests' seats. In terms of the aspects of presentation within the dining room, this is the most impressive form of service.

2. **Russian service.** With this form of service, the food is perfectly cooked in the kitchen, cut, placed onto a serving plate, and beautifully garnished. Then the dish is presented to the guests and served individually to everyone. Russian service can be used at a banquet or a dinner party.

3. **American service.** This is a simplified version of Russian service techniques. The food is prepared and dished onto individual plates in the kitchen, carried into the dining room, and served to the guests. The advantage of this technique is that it does not take as much time to serve; the guests can therefore enjoy the flavors and plate arrangement intended by the chef. American service looks easy; however, since it calls for all the guests at the table to be served at the same time even if they have ordered different dishes, it requires smooth, effective cooperation between the staff in the dining room and the staff in the kitchen.

Service staff should learn all three serving methods so that they can adjust to each situation as needed. American service is the most commonly used method today because guests are interested in the chef's talent and originality. They prefer a flavorful meal that is plated and colorfully arranged by him or her.

2

Restaurant Service Staff and Their Work

In the restaurant, service staff are responsible for the guest's satisfaction. Good service and unique food presentation enhance the guests' enjoyment of the atmosphere of the restaurant and the meal. This sense of responsibility should be deeply ingrained in the mind of every service staff member, who should work to improve his or her abilities so that the restaurant may be regarded as an excellent place to relax and enjoy oneself. Such a reputation will also enhance the status of the service staff.

Organization of the Restaurant Service Staff and Their Work

The size and responsibilities of a restaurant's service staff depend on the size and nature of the restaurant itself. For example, some restaurants may not have a bartender or a wine steward, and another staff member must take responsibility for that position. A general organizational scheme for service staff is as follows:

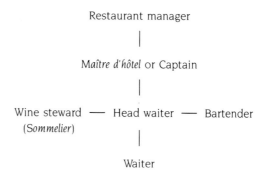

Restaurant Manager

The restaurant manager is in charge of the restaurant and its operation. The manager's daily work includes financial administration, the employment and training of staff, and discussion of both menu and prices with the chef in charge of the cooking staff. The manager also negotiates with companies that deal with the restaurant, such as food suppliers. He is not actually a member of the service staff, but he supervises the *maître d' hôtel* or Captain.

Maître d'hôtel or Captain

The *maître d'hôtel* is responsible for all service staff. He or she welcomes the guests, shows them to their tables, and takes orders. The *maître d'hôtel* takes extra care of the customers, and when necessary carves and *flambés*. He or she also works as a mediator between service and kitchen staff to maintain good relations and deals with guests' complaints. The *maître d'hôtel* controls the positioning of the staff and oversees their performance.

Head Waiter

The head waiter is usually responsible for serving the guests. A restaurant may have more than one head waiter, with each in charge of two or three tables only. Usually the head waiter performs the carving or *flambéing*.

Waiter

The waiter assists the head waiter by going back and forth between the kitchen and dining room, bringing out the ordered meals and taking away finished meals.

Wine Steward or Sommelier

The wine steward is in charge of all wine-related services in the dining room. He takes orders at the guests' tables and oversees the stocking of the wine cellar.

Bartender

The bartender is responsible for the mixing and serving of cocktails, apéritifs, and liqueurs.

The Service Staff

Guidelines for Service Staff

Personal Appearance

The appearance of the service staff greatly influences the atmosphere of the restaurant. Staff members should be neat and well groomed. Their nails should be kept short, and their shoes should be polished.

Each restaurant supplies its own uniform to the staff. Basically, men wear a white shirt, black pants, a jacket, and black shoes. Women wear a clean apron with the uniform, and their hairstyle, makeup, and nail polish must be conservative. Staff members should not wear perfume, cologne, or showy accessories. Service staff carry a large serving napkin, order pad, waiter's knife, and a box of matches, if necessary.

Attitude

Service staff members must be positive, healthy people to serve in their demanding positions. They are constantly on the move all day and must always keep smiling even when they are tired. Ideally, service staff members will be agile and elegant in their movements. Of course, they also must be skilled at using a knife in order to carve in front of guests.

The impression of the restaurant that guests receive depends upon the manner of the person who serves them. Therefore, service staff must always try to welcome and serve guests with sincerity and politeness. It is inexcusable for them to behave arrogantly to the guests, to talk to them in a very familiar tone, or to interrupt guests' conversation. It is often said that guests consider the ideal service staff to be much like air— absolutely necessary but never obvious.

There are many types of guests in the restaurant— young, old, high society, people who are difficult to please, and many others. To adjust effectively to their requests, and sometimes to deal with their complaints, service staff members should be trained to use their good sense and their knowledge of the cuisine and techniques of service. Finally, if they work as a team, not only with the other staff in the dining room but also with kitchen staff, their work place will surely be an excellent restaurant of high standards that offers smooth and efficient service.

3

Preliminary Arrangements for Welcoming Guests

Table Setting

There are two standard table settings. The à la carte setting is usually used in the restaurant. The full-course setting is used for prearranged meals.

À la Carte Setting

① Lay the plate about 1 inch (2 or 3 cm) from the table edge. This plate is ornamental and is not used. Some restaurants have custom plates made for this purpose. Plates with a restaurant symbol on the rim should be placed so that the symbol is at the top. This plate may be taken away before the first course or left until the main course is brought (in which case a consommé cup or an hors d'oeuvre dish is placed on it).

② The meat knife is placed to the right of the plate with its blade facing inward, and the fork is placed on the left. There are two ways to place the fork: English style, tines facing upward, or French style, tines facing downward. If the guest orders a fish dish, the cutlery should be changed. In all other cases, leave the cutlery and, when necessary, supply an extra fork and knife according to the dish ordered.

③ Place the bread plate to the left of the fork. Line up the bottom edge with the bottom edge of the service plate. Place the butter knife on the right edge of the butter plate.

④ Set the red wine glass about 1 inch (2 or 3 cm) above the end of the knife; put the water glass a little higher on its left. Or line up the glasses according to the wines ordered.

⑤ Put the napkin on the service plate. You may also decorate the table with flowers.

Full-Course Setting

For a full-course meal, place the service and bread plates as for the à la carte setting. The layout of the table is as follows: knives and spoons to the right of the ornamental plate, going from right to center in order of use; forks to the left of the plate, going from left to center in order of use; cutlery for dessert at the top of the plate. Line up the white wine, red wine, water, and champagne glasses diagonally from the right. Place the butter dish, salt and pepper, and ashtrays.

1. hors d'oeuvre knife
2. soup spoon
3. fish knife
4. dinner knife
5. service plate
6. napkin
7. dinner fork
8. fish fork
9. hors d'oeuvre fork
10. butter knife
11. bread plate
12. dessert knife
13. dessert fork
14. dessert spoon
15. white wine glass
16. red wine glass
17. water glass
18. champagne glass
19. salt shaker
20. pepper shaker
21. ashtray
22. butter dish

Tablecloth

How to Spread a Tablecloth

Stand between two legs of the table (along the longer side if the table is oblong).

1. Spread an undercloth (a thick flannel or thin sheet of spongelike material) or silencer on the table and fasten it with tacks. The undercloth will prevent the tablecloth from slipping, and will keep dishes from making noise when they are set down.

2. Place a tablecloth (folded in 16 as shown below) on the table with one folded edge along the right side. Unfold it once so that it hangs down on the right side of the table. Bring the folded edge of the cloth to the center line of the table.

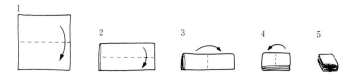

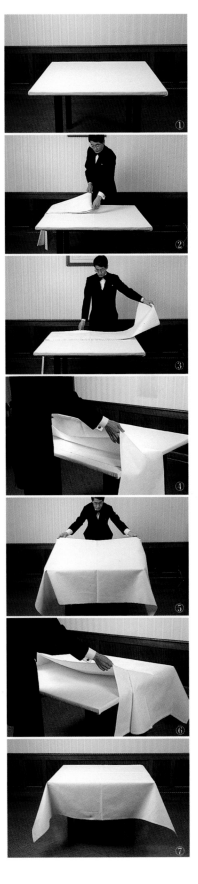

③ Unfold it in the opposite direction, to the left.

④ Lift an upper edge with the thumb and index finger and a second edge with the index and middle fingers.

⑤ Extend your arm to the other side of the table and let the bottom edge fall down.

⑥ Bring the center fold to the center of the table. Pull the edge of the tablecloth and let it hang.

⑦ Check that the tablecloth is straight and smooth.

Large tables for a buffet must be covered with several tablecloths. Place the creases so that all of the tablecloths look like one big cloth.

How to Spread the Top Cloth

In some restaurants a small tablecloth called a top cloth is used on top of the tablecloth. It may be a different color to coordinate with the decor. The top cloth can be changed easily when it is soiled.

① Unfold the top cloth, folded in quarters, standing at the corner of the table so that the center fold falls on the diagonal on the table.

② Check to see that the top cloth covers equally and that it is not wrinkled.

How to Remove the Tablecloth

③ Lift up the center line of the cloth.

④ Bring together the two edges that are hanging down, folding the cloth in two. Fold in half again.

⑤ Fold the tablecloth in half again in the other direction.

How to Change the Tablecloth

If you need to remove a stained tablecloth in front of guests, place the clean cloth over the table at the same time in order to hide the undercloth. First, lift up the center line of the tablecloth as in step 1 of "How to Remove the Tablecloth." Then follow steps 2–5 of "How to Spread the Tablecloth." Pull the edge of the new cloth and the center line of the old cloth toward you at the same time. Pull away the old cloth.

The Linen

Table linens include the tablecloth, the undercloth or silencer, the top cloth, the napkin, and the dish towel.

For the tablecloth, white or a solid light color is the most appropriate choice. Tablecloth fabrics include linen, hemp, cotton, and synthetic fiber. Among these, linen is regarded as the best because of its glossy texture and its durability. Napkins are generally of the same material and color as the tablecloth. All table linens must be kept clean and pressed.

Preparation of Plates and Cutlery

Glasses, dishes, and cutlery should be well polished with a dry napkin before they are placed on the table.

To Polish Cutlery

① With the left hand, hold each piece by its handle using a serving napkin. ② With another napkin, carefully wipe the piece so that it has no smudges on its surface from the tip to the handle.

To Polish Glasses

③ With the left hand, hold each glass by its base, using a serving napkin. With another napkin, polish the inside of the glass as well as the outside. ④ Next, polish the base and stem.

To Polish Dishes

⑤ Polish both sides of the dishes carefully with a serving napkin. ⑥ Avoid leaving fingerprints on the presentation side. ⑦ Stack the dishes and carry them covered with the serving napkin, being careful not to touch them with your body or fingers.

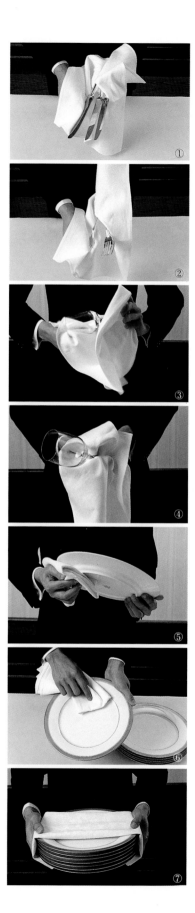

Folding the Napkins

You may fold the napkin simply in thirds or quarters and set it on the service plate, or you may use one of the many more decorative folding methods. The following list and accompanying photo illustrate several.

① Peach ② Buffet server ③ Cinderella ④ Wave
⑤ Crown ⑥ Folding Fan ⑦ Bird of paradise
⑧ Bishop's hat

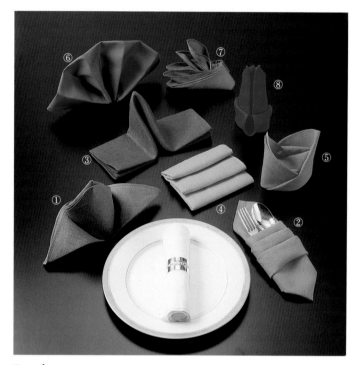

Peach

1. Fold the napkin in half diagonally.

2. Bring the lower right and left edges up to the top. Fold in half: bring bottom edge under top edge.

3. Fold the lower edges over the center. Slip the left inside the right.

4. Turn the napkin over.

5. Pull down both sides and make the shape neat.

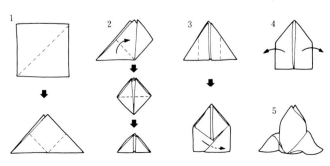

Wave

1. Fold the napkin lengthwise into thirds.

2. Fold the right edge (one-sixth of the length) over the center twice.

3. Repeat as in step 2 with the left side.

4. Fold the right side under the left.

5. You have three folded edges on the right side. Holding the bottommost folded edge with the right hand and the other two edges with the left hand, separate them so that three waves are created.

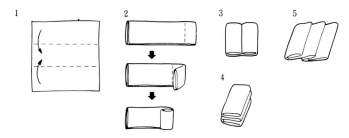

Crown

1. Fold the napkin in half to make a rectangle.

2. Fold the top right corner (b) down to the bottom edge (d) and bring the bottom corner (c) up to top center (a).

3. Turn the napkin over and bring the bottom over the top, leaving a triangle free.

4. Pull down another triangle. Turn upside down.

5. Fold the right quarter of the napkin toward the center, tucking the edge under the long fold.

6. Turn the napkin over. On this side, repeat step 5. Stand the napkin up and make it neat.

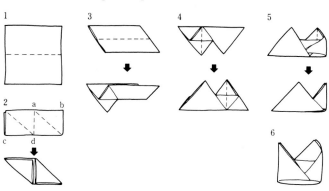

Folding Fan

1. Fold the napkin lengthwise into thirds.

2–3. Starting at the right, make accordion pleats.

4. Make a fan on the lower length and set on a plate.

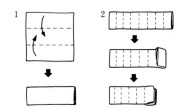   

Buffet Server

1. Fold the napkin into quarters.

2. Place the napkin so that the free corners are at the upper right. Roll down the top layer until just past the center.

3. Fold down the second layer and put its point under the first roll.

4. Fold the third layer in the opposite direction. You now have three equal rolls at the center of the napkin.

5. Fold under the upper left side and bottom right side.

Bird of Paradise

1. Fold the napkin into quarters.

2. Place it so that the free corners are at the bottom. Fold in half, bringing the bottom over the upper.

3. Fold the right and left sides to the center.

4. Fold the bottom triangles under.

5. Fold the napkin in half, bringing the left side under.

6. Lay the napkin so that the center fold is on top. Pull up the layers to form petals.

Cinderella

1. Fold the top and bottom edges of the napkin to the center. Fold in half (on line a–b).

2. Holding the center of the top edge with your fingers, fold down the right and left sides.

3. Fold up the bottom rectangle edges.

4. Turn the napkin over and fold in half.

5. Open the top and bottom edges.

6. Stand the napkin up and make the form neat.

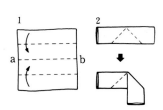
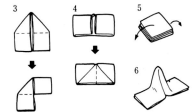

Bishop's Hat

1. Fold the napkin in half diagonally to form a triangle. Place it so that the free corner is on top.

2. Fold up the right and left edges to the top center.

3. Fold up the bottom point to within one-fourth or one-fifth the length of the top point.

4. Fold the point just folded in step 3 back to the bottom edge.

5. Turn it over and fold the left side toward the center.

6. Fold the right side over the left side, tucking its point into the left.

7. Stand the napkin up and make the form neat.

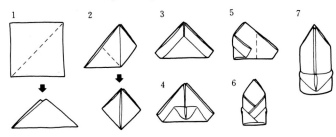

Flower Decoration

Floral arrangements on the dining table strike a festive and congenial note. Seasonal arrangements can be particularly appealing (for example, fir and pinecones for the winter holidays). Although flowers are an important element in the creation of a superior restaurant atmosphere, they should not detract from the meal. Arrangements should not be so tall that the seated guests cannot see each other. Strong-scented flowers should not be used, since they may interfere with the aromas of the meal. Do not use flowers whose pollen can disperse or whose petals fall off easily.

The assortment of flowers used in the arrangement depends on your taste; however, flowers in warm colors are a good choice because they enhance the look of the table and also improve the guests' appetite. Incorporate a sense of the season. Nuts or berries can be used as accents in autumn, and a flower floating in a bowl of water can provide a refreshing accent in summer.

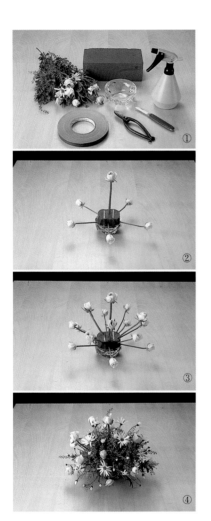

The choice of a vase depends on decor and table size. It is not necessary to use a silver vase. Bowls and cups are fine as long as they are deep enough for the sponge. At a small table (for two or four persons), freshly cut flowers can be placed in a glass without a sponge.

You can make your own original flower decorations by following the instructions below. Use a synthetic sponge, arranging flowers on every side, so that every guest at the table can appreciate it.

Round Style

1. Materials: flowers, vase, sponge, flower scissors, knife, spray bottle, and floral tape (see Photo ①).
2. Cut the sponge to fit the vase. Leave some room around the sponge to allow you to add water when it gets dry. So, even when a round vase is used, the sponge should be cut square. Its height should be about two fingers above the top of the vase. Place the sponge in the vase and attach it with floral tape. Avoid placing tape over the center of the sponge.

3. Place a flower in the center of the sponge. Keep in mind that the height of the arrangement should be about 6 inches (25 cm). Cut another 14 flowers the same length. Cut the stems obliquely for easy insertion into the sponge, $\frac{1}{2}$ to $\frac{3}{4}$ inch (1.5 to 2 cm) deep.

4. Place another flower directly in front of you, parallel with the surface of the table.

5. On the same plane as the second flower, equally space four more to form the bottom outline of your arrangement (see Photo ②).

6. Place five flowers, one between each two flowers of the bottom outline. Add five more at the same intervals as in step 5, but place them in the top of the sponge (see Photo ③). The framework of the round arrangement is made of these 15 flowers.

7. Fill in the gaps with the remaining five flowers.

8. Use foliage and other plants with very small flowers to hide the sponge (see Photo ④).

9. Spray with water to keep fresh. With occasional watering, the flowers will last four or five days.

Horizontal Style

1. Follow steps 1 and 2 for the "Round Style."

2. Place the nicest flower in the center. Remember that the height of the arrangement should be about

6 inches (25 cm), and its length should be one-third the length of the table. Place eight flowers around the center flower to form a rhombic outline along the bottom of the arrangement. Place six more flowers, using as a guide the flower outline

Sautéed frog legs

Dessert knife, dessert fork, and finger bowl (see Photo ④)

Bouillabaisse

Fish knife, fish fork, and soup spoon (see Photo ⑤). Plate for waste will also be placed to the side of the table settings.

Lobster or crayfish

Fish knife, fish fork, lobster cracker, lobster fork, finger bowl, plate for waste (see Photo ⑥)

Spaghetti

Fork (placed to the right of the napkin) and a container of Parmesan cheese (see Photo ⑦)

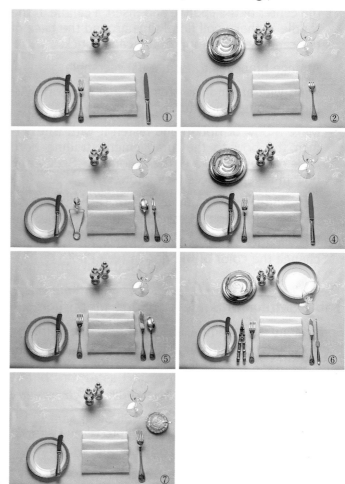

Restaurant Service Utensils

The service utensils used in a restaurant consist of serving utensils and table utensils for the guests. Glittering, polished glasses, knives, and forks produce a refined atmosphere at the table. Ice buckets, dish warmers, and carts are utensils that impress the guests even more. Therefore, it is important that these utensils be properly maintained. The maintenance of these utensils depends upon the quality, use, and design of the utensil and the materials used to make it. Each waiter must be familiar with proper maintenance methods and must keep the utensils presentable at all times. For example, knives should be sharpened regularly so that they will be ready to be used at any time.

Serving Utensils

Table and wine service utensils The following utensils are shown in the photo on page 34.

① Crumb remover (*pelle à miettes*)

② Wine basket (*panier à vin*)

③ Crumb sweeper (*ramasse-miettes*): To use this type of sweeper, you simply slide it across the table, and automatically the crumbs are picked up by an inner rotating brush and stored inside.

④ Wine-tasting cup (*taste-vin* or *tâte-vin*): This utensil is a shallow, small vessel used for wine tasting by the *sommelier*. The uneven bottom allows you to see the depth of color at first sight and allows the wine to breathe.

⑤ Ice bucket or wine cooler, champaign bucket (*seau à champagne*)

⑥ Waiter's corkscrew (*couteau limonadier*): This essential utensil for the *sommelier* contains a knife for cutting off the foil covering the neck of the wine bottle, a corkscrew for drawing the cork out, and a bottle opener. It folds for easy storage.

⑦ Dish warmer (*réchaud*): This photo shows the dish warmer with lamps used for heating a dish at the table. There is also a dish warmer that can heat at higher temperatures and is suitable for flambéing (see item ⑦ in the photo on page 35). To retain the warmth of a dish, use an electric dish warmer or a dish warmer with a plate over the lamps to soften the thermal conduction.

34

Copper service utensils   Ornate copper service utensils are often used for a buffet or banquet. If you neglect to polish copper utensils regularly, the surface, which has characteristic brilliance, will become dark and iridescent. The following utensils are shown in the photos on page 35.

① Sauce boat (*sauciére*)

② Butter pot (*beurrier*)

③ Oval casserole (*cocotte*)

④ Fish board with cover (*planche de présentation avec couvercle—motif poisson*)

⑤ Small saucepan (*casserolette*): This utensil is used for serving a garnish or sauce.

⑥ Saucepan (*casserole*)

⑦ Dish warmer (*réchaud*)

⑧ Sauté pan (*poêle*)

⑨ Vegetable dish with cover (*légumier*): This utensil is used for serving a garnish such as vegetables. Items ⑩ and ⑬ are large dishes of the same type and are used mainly for banquets or buffets in which various dishes are served.

⑩ Vegetable dish with cover (*légumier*)

⑪ Fish kettle (*poissonnière*)

⑫ Oval casserole (*cocotte*)

⑬ Vegetable dish with cover (*légumier*)

⑭ Dish warmer/chafing dish (*réchaud*)

Knives for service Various kinds of knives and a special fork are required for carving and boning. Knives should be chosen according to the carving task being undertaken and the ingredients, size, and method of food preparation. It is convenient to have both a small and large knife of the same kind, so that you may choose the size required for the task. Each utensil has unique characteristics and intended uses that should be understood by restaurant personnel. The following knives are shown in the photo on page 36.

① Carving fork (*fourchette*): Used to support meat when carving large pieces. If you need to be more precise, use a serving fork with four tines.

② Paring knife (*couteau d'office*): A small knife suitable for paring fruits or for cutting small ingredients.

③ Fish-filleting knife (*couteau à filets de sole*): The blade of this knife bends easily; it is used mainly for filleting fish with thin meat, such as sole. It may also be used to cut thin slices of meat from duck by running the blade along the curve of the breast.

④ Chef's knife (*couteau éminceur*): This knife has many uses (such as carving chicken, cutting fruits, etc.).

⑤ ⑥ Boning knife (*couteau à désosser*): These knives are used for boning or carving chicken. The steady grip and short, tough blade allow for strong carving.

⑦ Carving knife (*couteau tranchelard*): This knife has a long, thin, narrow blade that makes it appropriate for slicing large pieces of meat (such as roast leg of lamb, ham, etc.).

⑧ ⑨ Ham slicing knife (*couteau à jambon*): These knives are suitable for slicing smoked salmon and cured ham. The grooves in the blade allow these knives to move smoothly without sticking to the meat. These knives are flexible and easy to use.

Carving boards A carving board is usually used for carving food in a restaurant. There are various styles and sizes, and some are more ornate than others; however, each carving board has a trench around its edge to catch the meat's juices. The following carving boards are shown in the marginal photos to the left.

① Carving board (*planche à découper*)

② Leg of lamb carving board (*Planche de présentation—motif gigot*)

Carts   The following service carts are shown in the accompanying photos.

① Carving trolley or roast beef cart (*voiture à trancher* or *chariot à rosbif*): This wagon is used for carving large pieces of meat, such as roast beef. If you slide the cover open, you will find the carving board and the container for warming the sauce. The rack nearest to you is set with carving knives, serving knife, and a carving fork. The folding rack to the right is a rest for the individual serving plates.

② Dessert cart (*chariot à desserts*): Cakes and desserts are arranged in the glass case and presented to the guests. The dessert is divided according to the guest's order and served on individual serving plates found on the tray below.

Silverware

In addition to knives, forks, and spoons, the silverware in a restaurant includes various utensils such as service platters, soup tureens, coffee pots, salt shakers, and pepper pots. The tableware most often used is made of silver-plated nickel or stainless steel, although some sterling silver is also used (this is almost pure silver with at least 5 percent added metal, such as copper, to make it more durable). Sterling silver is highly valued not only for its rarity but also for its shine and ability to resist rust; however, it does tarnish easily.

Silver-plated nickel (an alloy of copper, nickel, and zinc plated with silver) has the appearance and quality of real silver, but without the tendency to tarnish.

Since certain foods can affect the condition of both sterling silver and silver-plated nickel, care should be taken to clean them with a mild detergent soon after use. Do not soak silverware in water for a long period of time. Use a soft cloth for drying, and dry thoroughly. If proper care is taken, you will only have to use a silver polish occasionally. It is also important to store the silverware properly. The more superior in quality the silver, the softer the material, and the more easily damaged.

Stainless steel, which contains a high percentage of nickel, has a protective outer layer that prevents it from tarnishing or rusting. However, scouring or scraping stainless steel can remove the protective layer, so always wash with a mild detergent and be sure to dry thoroughly.

Large-sized silver service utensils The following utensils are shown in the marginal photos to the left and the photos on page 39.

① Round service platter (*plat de présentation rond*)

② Oval service platter (*plat de présentation ovale*)

③ Fish dish with cover (*plat à poisson avec couvercle*): An inner plate with holes is attached to this utensil so as to drain the moisture from food. This utensil is suitable for serving poached fish.

④ Vegetable dish with cover (*légumier*)

5. Bread basket (*corbeille à pain*)
6. Teapot (*théière*)
7. Sauce boat (*saucière*)
8. Coffeepot (*cafetière*)
9. Soup tureen (*soupière*)
10. Water pot (*pot à eau*)

Table service utensils   The following utensils are shown in the accompanying photo.

① Finger bowl (*rince-doigts*)

② Mustard dish (*moutardier*)

③ Pepper mill (*mouilin à poivre*)

④ Salt shaker (*salière*)

⑤ Pepper pot or shaker (*poivrier*)

⑥ Butter dish with cover (*beurrier avec couvercle*)

⑦ Coaster for bottles (*dessous-de-bouteille*)

⑧ Oil and vinegar set (*huilier-vinaigrier*)

⑨ Ashtray (*cendrier*)

40

Service cutlery   The following cutlery items are used when serving guests. Use your own judgment when choosing the cutlery that is most convenient for the task. The name of the item does not necessarily dictate its use. For example, you can use the ice cream serving spoon for serving the fish. The following items are shown in the accompanying photo.

① Soup ladle (*louche à potage*)

② Fish serving fork (*fourchette à servir le poisson*)

③ Fish serving knife (*couteau à servir le poisson*)

④ Carving fork (*fourchette à découper*)

⑤ Carving knife (*couteau à découper*)

⑥ Cake server (*pelle à gâteau*)

⑦ Pie server (*pelle à tarte*)

⑧ Ice cream serving spoon (*cuiller à servir la glace*)

⑨ Lobster cracker (*pince à homard*): This utensil is used for cracking or breaking the claw shells of lobster. When you take the meat out of the shell, use the lobster fork (see item ⑩).

⑩ Lobster fork (*fourchette à homard*)

⑪ Cheese knife (*couteau à fromage*)

⑫ Snail tongs (*pince à escargots*)

⑬ Snail fork (*fourchette à escargots*)

⑭ Sugar spoon (*cuiller à sucre*)

⑮ Sauce ladle (*cuiller à sauce*)

⑯ Salad serving fork (*fourchette à servir la salade*)

⑰ Salad serving spoon (*cuiller à servir la salade*)

Cutlery for guests The following cutlery items are used by the guests. They are shown in the accompanying photo.

① Sauce spoon (*cuiller à sauce*)

② Demitasse spoon (*cuiller à sauce*)

③ Teaspoon (*cuiller à café*)

④ Ice cream spoon (*cuiller à glace*)

⑤ Dessert spoon (*cuiller à dessert*)

⑥ Oyster fork (*fourchette à huîtres*)

⑦ Pastry fork (*fourchette à gâteau*)

⑧ Butter knife or Butter spreader (*couteau tartineur*)

⑨ Bouillon spoon (*cuiller à consommé*)

⑩ Tablespoon (*grand cuiller*)

⑪ Dessert fork (*fourchette à dessert*)

⑫ Dessert knife (*couteau à dessert*)

⑬ Fish fork (*fourchette à poisson*)

⑭ Fish knife (*couteau à poisson*)

⑮ Dinner fork (*grande fourchette*)

⑯ Dinner knife (*grande couteau*)

Glasses

Basic glasses   These glasses are shown in the photo that follows.

① Champagne glass (*verre à champagne*)
② Water glass (goblet) (*verre à eau*)
③ Red wine glass (*verre à vin rouge*)
④ White wine glass (*verre à vin blanc*)

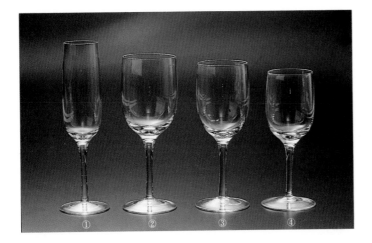

Various wine glasses   These glasses are shown in the photo that follows.

① Bordeaux wine glass (*verre à bordeaux*)
② Burgundy balloon glass (*verre ballon à bourgogne*)
③ Alsace wine glass (*verre à vin d'Alsace*)
④ Sherry glass (*verre à xérès*)

Various kinds of glasses These glasses are shown in the photo that follows.

① Cocktail glass (*verre à cocktail*)
② Brandy glass (*verre à spiritueux*)
③ Liqueur glass (*verre à liqueur*)
④ Highball or tall glass (*verre à long-drinks*)
⑤ Fruit juice glass (*verre à jus de fruits*)
⑥ Old-fashioned or whiskey glass (*verre à whisky*)

4

Service in the Dining Room

Serving Techniques

There are four standard methods of serving. Each restaurant chooses the method most appropriate to its size, nature, number of guests, and cuisine.

Plate Service

The most common serving method is plate service: The food is placed on individual plates in the kitchen and carried out to each guest. Serve each guest quickly and courteously, without bending over the dish or turning your back to the guest. (Ordinarily, women are served first.)

Entrées may be served from the guest's right using your right hand (Photo ①) or, preferably, from the guest's left side using your left hand (Photo ②). All other dishes, including the salad plate, the bread and butter plate, and the finger bowl should be placed on the guest's left side. You should not serve a dish from the guest's left side using your right hand (see Photo ③), as you may elbow the guest. Serve drinks or remove used plates from the guest's right side using your right hand.

Russian Service

For the Russian service method, the dish is presented to the guests first and then served onto individual plates. First, place the serving plate containing the food on a side table next to the dining table. Next, place the individual plates, which have been warmed or cooled according to the food, before the guests. Hold the serving plate in your left hand with a service napkin, and serve from the guest's left using a serving spoon and fork. This method is used for banquets and similar events.

French Service

The most impressive method, French service, is one in which the food is served to the guests after having been presented and prepared at the table (see Photo ④). Place the food, sauce, seasonings, and utensils on a side table next to the dining table (or carry the required items on a cart from the kitchen into the dining room). Set the individual plates to the right of the serving dish, arrange the food attractively on each plate, and serve using the procedure outlined for plate service. If the dish is hot, place it on a warmer. This superb method of serving can be very gratifying to the guests; it does, however, require adequate space and service staff with suitable skills.

American Service

American service combines the advantages of plate service and French service. The food is individually plated in the kitchen, carried out on a serving tray, and placed on a side table next to the dining table. The plates are then served to the guests using the same procedure as for plate service. If you use a dish or banquet cover, place the plates on the serving tray and put the dish covers over the food. Position the tray properly on the side table (Photo ①). Place the plate before the guest using the plate service rules, and take the cover off gently (Photo ②).

How to Hold Plates

To hold one plate, place your thumb on the edge of the plate so as not to leave fingerprints. Support the bottom with your other fingers (Photo ①). There are three basic methods of holding two plates:

1. Support the bottom of the first plate with the inner three fingers of the left hand and place the thumb and little finger on the plate (see Photo ②). Place the second plate over the first and rest it on the thumb, the little finger, and the wrist (Photo ③).

2. Place the thumb of the left hand on the edge of the plate and support the bottom with the index and middle finger. Do not let the ring finger or little finger touch the plate (Photo ④). Place the second plate over the first and support it with the thumb, ring finger, little finger, and wrist (Photo ⑤).

3. Hold the first plate as in method 2 (Photo ⑥). Slide the second plate between the first plate and the middle finger, supporting it with the ring and little fingers.

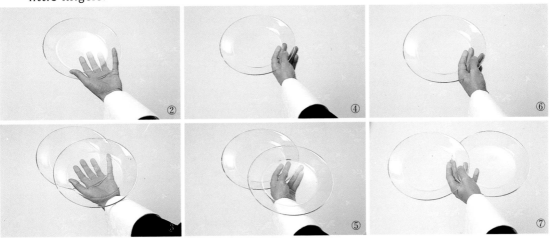

Follow these steps when holding three plates:
① Hold the first plate as in method 2.
② Slide the second plate between the first plate and the index finger. Use the middle finger and ring finger to support it.
③ Place the third plate on top of the others, and support it on the thumb, little finger, and wrist.

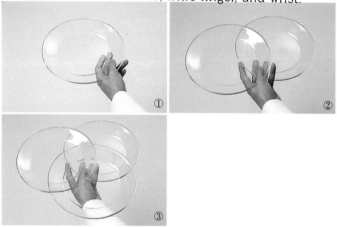

How to Remove the Plates

Remove the plate from the guest's right. For more than two plates, shift them to the left hand and stack them one at a time. There are two methods of removing plates. They correspond with methods 1 and 2 on page 47. Using method 1:

① Remove the first plate with your right hand, transfer it to the left hand, and hold it as in method 1. Place the knife and fork across the plate.
② Place the second plate on your left hand. Place the second fork beside the first on the first plate. Move any leftovers onto the lower plate with the knife. Place the knife under the fork handles.
③ Place the third plate on the empty second plate. Put the fork and knife on the third plate.

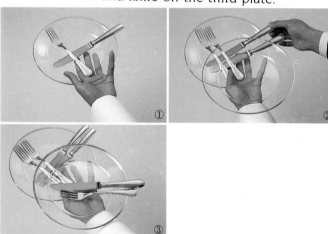

Using method 2:
① Remove the first plate with the right hand, transfer it to the left hand, and hold it as in method 2. Place the knife and fork across the plate.
② Place the second plate on your left hand.
③ Shift the fork and any leftovers to the lower plate.
④ Place the second knife on the lower plate.

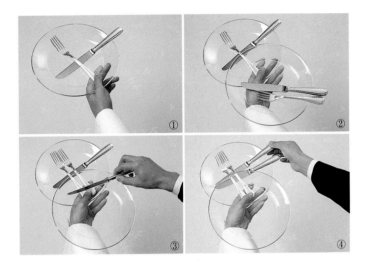

How to Carry and Hold Glasses

Carry glasses on a tray lined with a service napkin to prevent slipping. When carrying many glasses, do not grip them by the stems, as the glasses may crack (Photo ①). Support the bottom of the tray with your flat palm and carry it steadily (Photo ②). Do not carry it on your fingertips (Photo ③). Each glass should be held individually by the stem (Photo ④). Do not grip the glass at the top (Photo ⑤) or grasp the rims of several glasses together (Photo ⑥).

Order of Precedence at the Table

When a special meal, such as a banquet or a dinner party, is held in the restaurant, you must serve the guests according to the order of precedence. First the seat of the hostess is determined and then the seat of the host. After that, the seats of the other invited guests are determined, taking into consideration their age and status.

If the guests are all men, the invited guest who ranks highest is seated where the hostess should be. The same rule applies when the guests are all women.

Traditionally, the hostess is seated at the upper seat and the host at the lower seat just opposite her. The upper seat is defined as the seat that is farthest from the door and allows one to look out over the whole restaurant with one's back to the wall. Opposite it is the lower seat. If the restaurant looks out onto a garden, the upper seat faces it. The opposite position is the lower seat.

The following illustration shows the two styles that guide order of precedence.

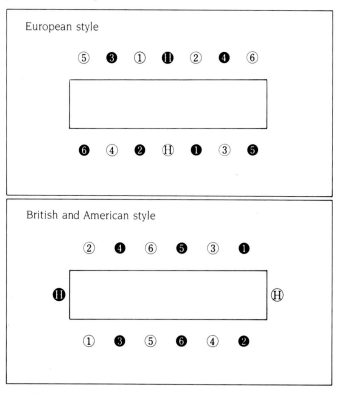

Usually women are served first. Begin serving with the highest-ranking woman on the right side of the host.

Next, serve the second-ranking woman on the left side of the host. Go around the table serving the other women in ranking order and finish by serving the hostess. Continue serving to the men in order also. Begin with the highest-ranking male guest and finish with the host.

Service Procedures

Only the basic techniques of serving have been discussed thus far. This section, however, details the entire procedure as carried out in an actual restaurant, from receiving guests to seeing them to the door.

Showing Guests into the Room

- Receive the guests at the door, and greet them with a warm smile (Photo ①).

- Confirm the guests' reservation and the number of guests to be seated. Escort them to the proper table (see Photo ②). For guests who have already reserved a table, escort them to their prepared table and seat them according to the order of precedence. For guests who have not reserved, the situation dictates the procedure. For example, a couple should be escorted to a table for two near the wall so that they can feel a sense of privacy. In the case of one guest, seat him or her at a table near a corner. When guests arrive with children, it is necessary to consider the location of their table so as not to disturb other guests.

- First help the women to take their seats. (As a general rule, women should be seated first. The "ladies first" rule applies to all the following services.) Pull

the chair out, allow the guest to sit, and then gently push the chair forward using your knees (Photo ③). Crumbs on the chair are displeasing; inspect all tables before receiving guests (Photo ④).

54

Bread service

- Put bread into a bread basket that contains a service napkin, and serve it from the guest's left.

White wine service

- Generally white wine is served with the hors d'oeuvres. Serve water to guests who do not drink wine.

- Wrap the bottle in a service napkin, and show it to the guest so that he or she can confirm that it is the correct selection (Photo ②).

- Pour a small quantity of wine into the host's glass and have him or her sample it (Photos ③ and ④). If the host approves, serve wine to the women first. Drinks are always served from the right. The guest who sampled the wine is the last one to be served.

Hors d'oeuvres

- Hors d'oeuvres stimulate the appetite. In Photo ⑤ plate service is being used.

Soup

- When serving clear soup, pour it into a consommé cup with handles (Photo ⑥). Pour other soups into a soup bowl (Photo ⑦). Bowls should be cooled or heated before serving. When you use the soup tureen, hold it with a service napkin in your left hand. Ladle the soup into the bowl from the guest's left side. The bowl should be about 80 percent full (one to two ladles of soup) (Photo ⑧).

Fish

- Lay the fish knife and fork on the table (Photo ①).
- Serve the fish using Russian service. Grasp it with a serving spoon and fork (Photos ③ and ④), and place it on the plate, being careful not to break it. Pour the sauce over the fish. (Photo ②).

Sherbet

- Between fish and meat dishes, serve plain sherbet to remove the aftertaste. Sherbet in a glass is placed on a saucer and carried out on a tray (Photo ⑤).

Red wine service

- Using a wine basket, follow the order of serving described for white wine (Photo ⑥).

Meat

- There are many methods of serving meat, one of which is to use a side table to carve the meat for the guests. While keeping the dish warm on a dish warmer, carve the meat (Photo ⑦) and place it quickly on a warm plate using a serving spoon and fork. Garnish meat on the plate (Photo ⑧), and serve it to the guest (Photo ⑨).

Salad

- When serving a small salad with a meat dish, move the bread plate forward and place the plate of salad on the table from the left side (Photo ①).

Removing plates

- When the guests finish eating, remove the plates from the right side using your right hand (Photo ②). Remove plates that are on the left side, such as bread plates, from the left.

- When you remove plates from several guests at one time, shift the first plate to the left hand. Push leftovers toward the edge of the plate using a knife, and lay forks and knives across the plate with the knife below. Remove the second plate (Photo ③) and place it on your left wrist. Place the second fork beside the first. Push leftovers gently onto

the edge of the first plate. Place the knife on the first plate. The same applies to the third or fourth plate. Placing knives and forks on the plate without any order can result in a very unsteady pile (Photo ④).

Cheese

- Present a variety of cheeses on a cart, and let the guest make a selection (Photo ⑤).

- Cut and divide the cheeses selected into proper sizes, and serve them on a plate (Photo ⑥).

Arranging the table

- Before serving dessert, remove unnecessary tableware (such as salt and pepper), leaving only the water glasses. Slide the crumb sweeper across the tablecloth, and arrange the table neatly (see Photo ⑦ on page 56).

Dessert

- Set a dessert spoon, fork, and knife on the table. You may also serve champagne or sweet white wine.

- Present a variety of cakes on a dessert cart, and let the guests make a selection (Photo ①).

- Cut the cake selected by the guest into the proper size, and serve it on a dessert plate (Photo ②). Make the pieces equal and pleasing to the eye.

Coffee

- Place a cream pitcher and a sugar bowl on the table. Also, place a demitasse cup and saucer in front of the guest with a demitasse spoon on the saucer.

- Pour coffee from the right (Photo ③).

Apéritifs and digestifs

- Apéritifs are served while the guests review the menu. Kir and sherry are popular apéritifs.

- Digestifs, also called cordials or liqueurs, are served after coffee.

Changing ashtrays

- When cigarettes have accumulated in the ashtray, exchange it for a clean one.

- To prevent scattering of ashes, hold two clean ashtrays in your right hand and place them on top of the used ashtray on the table. Pick up the stack and move it to your left hand. Remove the top ashtray and place it on the table.

Helping Guests Leave Their Seats

- Stand behind the guest's chair, holding the top with both hands. Allow the guest to stand up, and pull the chair back gently (Photo ④). Thank the guests for coming, and see them to the door.

5

Attractive Service Techniques

Carving and Flambéing

This basic principle should guide a restaurant's service:
Guests should eat the food when it is at its best. If you
use any of the methods of service mentioned before
(in which foods are served on individual plates; served
by the waiter from the serving plate onto each guest's
plate; or carved and arranged at the tableside), you
should always keep this principle in mind. Moreover, it
is important that the service provided allow the guests
to enjoy their meal to the fullest.

To achieve such results, the service must be visually
pleasing, and a most impressive effect is achieved by
serving methods involving carving and finishing the
dishes at tableside. Because these techniques require
the waiter to finish the dish in the presence of the
guests, he or she must be as knowledgeable as the
chef concerning the ingredients, techniques, and presentation of the food.

In this section we will concentrate mainly on two tableside techniques, carving and flambéing. It is assumed
that only one waiter is serving, even though he or she
is often assisted by another waiter in arranging the
carved foods on plates and serving them to the guests.
This facilitates effective and efficient service.

Carving

An impressive dish, such as a large piece of roasted
meat or a whole fish, is first presented to the guests
and then served carved.

When carving food, speed is extremely important. For
hot dishes you must prepare the dish warmer on a
side table and keep your carving and individual plates
warm, so that the foods do not get cold. For cold foods
you must chill the plates ahead of time.

You must also consider the number of servings needed
and the quantity of each serving. When the quality
and volume of meat vary according to the part of the
animal it comes from, as it does with chicken and
fish, arrange equal amounts of meat from the various
parts on each individual plate. To carry out the carving effectively, and thus to allow the guests to enjoy
their meal to the fullest, a knowledge of the ingredients, the method of preparation, and the best way to
carve and present is essential. For example, beef and

lamb, which are enjoyed with their delicious juices, are held with the flat of a fork while carving, so as not to allow too much of the juice to escape. The fundamental utensils for carving are a serving spoon, a serving fork, and a knife appropriate to the task. It is essential that the waiter become adept at using the serving spoon and knife and be able to choose the proper knives (see p. 36).

The performance and skill of the waiter in carving the food become a point of interest for the guests. In order to be adequately prepared for this task, you may need constant practice.

Flambéing

Brandy, which has a high alcohol content, is often poured over food and ignited. The beauty of the flames and the rich aroma of the brandy add to the atmosphere at the table. The aroma and flavor of the brandy are also absorbed by the food, enhancing its taste.

To serve flambéed foods while they are hot, you must warm the plates as you do when serving carved foods; prepare a dish warmer whose heat output is higher than an ordinary one. Place all that you need conveniently on a side table. Since this serving technique is meant to be an attractive display, you may choose to use different utensils from those you would use if you were preparing the dish in the kitchen.

For flambéing, thoroughly preheat the pan that contains the foods. Be sure to remove the pan from the heat before you pour in the spirits, to prevent the fire from suddenly blazing up. Only a small amount of spirits is needed to produce a brilliant flame.

The remainder of this chapter details carving, finishing, serving, and presentation methods for a wide variety of dishes. These dishes are presented by category: hors d'oeuvres, fish, meat, garnished dishes, and desserts. The chapter concludes with a discussion of the various types of cheese and the appropriate methods of serving them.

Caviar

(*Caviar*)

* **Note:** Caviar also can be served Russian-style with blinis (thin buckwheat sourdough pancakes) and sour cream, or diced hardboiled eggs and finely chopped onion or parsley may be added to the caviar according to the guest's taste.

Utensils: two teaspoons for serving caviar

Ingredients: caviar, melba toast, lemon

Caviar is salted roe of sturgeon, differing in size and color depending on the kind of sturgeon: The largest-grained and highest-graded are beluga and ossetra, and the smallest-grained is sevruga.

1 Spoon out the caviar. Use an additional spoon to form the caviar into a neat pile on the plate.

PRESENTATION: Garnish with melba toast and lemon.*

SPECIAL UTENSILS: You may serve caviar with the can. Place it in a bowl of cracked ice, or use special serving dishes, also with cracked ice.

Ham

(Jambon cuit)

Kitchen preparation: Carefully place the inside of the ham leg down.

Utensils: paring knife, carving knife, serving spoon, fork

1 Holding the bone with a wrapped napkin, remove the fatty portion of the ham.

2 Make a circular cut around the bone end. Diagonally cut thin slices.

3 Remove the fatty portions and arrange slices on a plate.

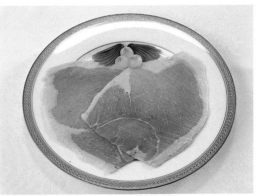

PRESENTATION: Garnish with pickled cucumber and small pickled onions.

Liver pâté

(Terrine de foie gras)

Utensils: pot containing hot water for warming the knife, two dinner knives, serving spoon, fork

Ingredients: liver pâté, chopped aspic (a clear jelly made from meat or fish stock), melba toast made of brioche

1 Warm a dinner knife in the hot water. (After each cut, reheat the knife in the hot water.)

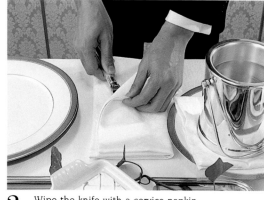

2 Wipe the knife with a service napkin.

3 Steadying the mold with your hand, cut the right edge of the pâté along the mold.

4 Continue cutting around the pâté.

5 Cut a thin slice of pâté. This first slice is not served to the guest.

6 Remove the slice, holding it with two knives.

7 Cut a slice about ⅜ inch (1 cm) thick.

8 Remove the slice from the mold and place it on the plate, holding it in shape with both knives as in step 6.

9 Cut off the butter that solidified over the top of the pâté.

PRESENTATION: Garnish with aspic and melba toast.

Smoked salmon

(Saumon fumé)

Utensils: ham-slicing knife, serving spoon, fork, plate for waste

Ingredients: smoked salmon, melba toast, capers, lemon, finely chopped onions

1 Begin slicing one-quarter of the way from the tail. Slice off the toughened outer skin.

2 Supporting the salmon with a fork, slice toward the tail the widest and thinnest piece possible.

3 Rotate the knife so that the salmon wraps around it.

4 Unroll and place on a plate.

5 Garnish with lemon.

PRESENTATION: Serve salmon with melba toast. Garnish with capers and chopped onion according to the guest's taste.

Cured ham

(Jambon cru)

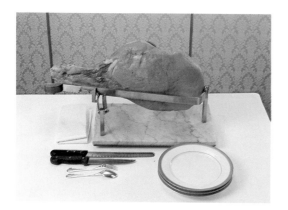

Utensils: ham-slicing knife, boning knife, serving spoon, fork, plate for the bone

A cured ham is salted and aged slowly while being dried; it is not heated or smoked.

1 Grip the leg bone with a service napkin, and begin slicing off the outside from the top using the boning knife.

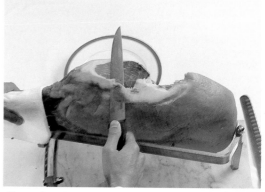

2 When the lean appears, slice off the skin and excess fat around the incision.

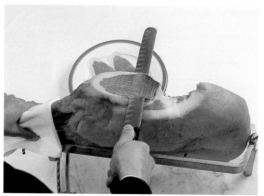

3 Move the ham-slicing knife back and forth to make paper-thin slices.

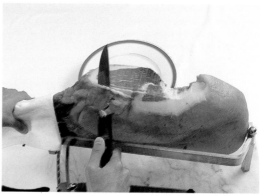

4 If the fat around the incision gets thicker, slice it off again.

Kitchen preparation: Place the ham on the holder so that the leg bone faces to the waiter's left and the side with more meat faces up.

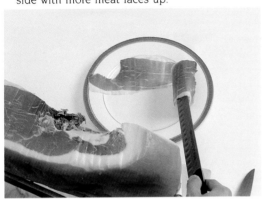

5 Wind the sliced ham around the ham-slicing knife and unroll it on the plate.

6 If the round bone appears, take it off using the boning knife.

7 Carve the ham into wide, thin slices. Continue slicing until you reach the femoral bone. Carve the other side of the ham in the kitchen.

PRESENTATION: Unroll each piece and spread it out on a plate as in step 5. The ham may be garnished with fruit, such as melon or fig, Italian-style.

Melon with cured ham
(Melon au jambon cru)

Utensils: filleting knife, chef's knife, serving spoon, fork, cutting plate, plate for seeds

1   Cut off the stem with the filleting knife.

2   Halve the melon with the chef's knife.

3   With the spoon, scoop out the seeds of the melon.

4   Divide each half into equal pieces with the chef's knife.

5 Separate half of the melon slice from the rind using the filleting knife and holding the melon with the fork.

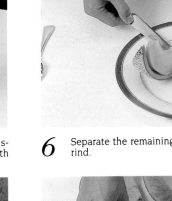

6 Separate the remaining half of the melon from the rind.

7 Halve the piece of melon.

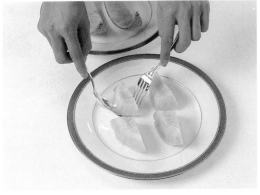

8 Place the melon on the plate with the serving spoon and fork.

PRESENTATION: Drape the ham over the pieces of melon.

Grapefruit

(*Pamplemousse*)

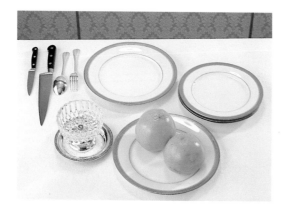

Utensils: paring knife, chef's knife, serving spoon, fork, cutting plate, plate for peel

FIRST METHOD

1 To steady the grapefruit, cut off the stem end of the peel using a chef's knife. Halve the grapefruit.

2 Remove the seeds with the end of a paring knife.

3 Separate each section by cutting between the peel and the flesh with the paring knife.

PRESENTATION: Place the grapefruit half in a fruit cocktail dish (a dish with a stem) or on a plate, and serve with a sugar bowl.

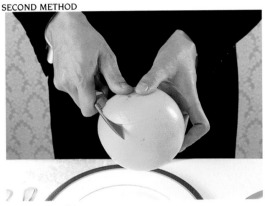

1 Make an incision in the peel around the stem using a paring knife.

2 Cut a little piece off the opposite end.

3 Pierce the cut peel with a serving fork and stab into the stem. Pare toward the incision so as not to leave the white peel.

4 Cut inside the membrane of each section.

5 Remove the sections of flesh. Leave the juice on the plate and pour it over the fruit on presentation.

PRESENTATION: Place in a fruit cocktail dish or on a plate and serve with a sugar bowl.

Lobster with hollandaise sauce

(Homard à la nage, sauce hollandaise)

Utensils: carving board, chef's knife, lobster cracker, serving spoon, fork, plate for waste

1 Lift the lobster out of the court bouillon using a serving spoon and fork.

2 Place the lobster on a service napkin to allow the liquid to drain.

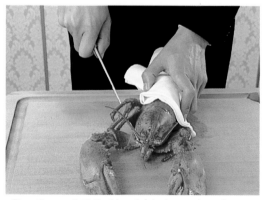

3 Place a chef's knife under the legs and cut the joints of the claws, supporting the trunk with the napkin.

4 Cut off the legs.

5 Supporting with the fork, slowly slide the right fillet off the backbone with the spoon.

6 Gently remove the left fillet so as not to break it.

7 Slide the spoon under the backbone from the head to the tail to lift it.

8 When you reach the base of the tail, remove the backbone and the tail. Place the bottom fillet on the guest's plate.

9 Place the fillets one on top of the other.

PRESENTATION: Garnish with boiled, salted potatoes, lemon, and beurre noisette (melted butter cooked till hazel-colored).

Grilled sole with anchovy butter

(Sole grillée, beurre d'anchois)

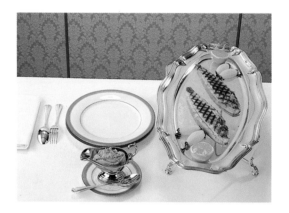

Utensils: dish warmer, serving spoon, fork, cutting plate, plate for waste

1 Cut off the head of the sole with a serving spoon. Supporting with a fork, remove the outer edges of the backbone with the spoon.

2 Run the spoon along the backbone toward the tail. Supporting with the fork, remove the right upper fillet from the backbone. Repeat with the left side.

3 Detach the backbone from the lower meat, lifting it with the spoon, and remove with the tail. Transfer the fillets to the individual serving plate.

PRESENTATION: Garnish with boiled, salted potatoes and lemon. Top with anchovy butter either melted, served in a sauce boat, or solid, in pats.

Colbert-style sole with maître d'hotel butter

(Sole Colbert, beurre maître d'hotel)

* **Maître d'hôtel butter**: Knead soft butter with finely chopped parsley and lemon juice.

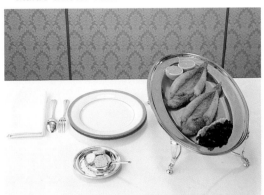

Utensils: dish warmer, serving spoon, fork, cutting plate, plate for waste

1 Cut off the head with a spoon, supporting with a fork. Run the spoon along the inside, making a small incision from the front to the base of the tail.

2 Run the spoon along the opposite edge as in step 1.

3 Insert the spoon beneath the backbone. Lift the backbone, holding it with the spoon and fork, and snap it off at the base of the tail.

PRESENTATION: Garnish with deep-fried parsley and lemon. Top with maître d'hôtel butter* in pats as shown here, or melted, served in a sauceboat.

Poached brill in saffron sauce

(Tronçon de barbue poché, sauce au safran)

Utensils: fish knife, serving spoon, fork, cutting plate, plate for waste

1 Place the brill on a service napkin in order to drain the liquid.

2 Strip off the white skin, using a fish knife and a fork.

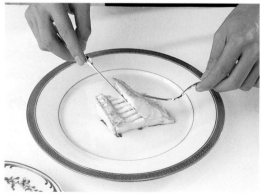

3 Insert the fish knife between the backbone and the meat, and remove the fillet. Place it on the individual serving plate using the serving spoon and fork.

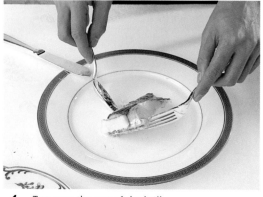

4 Turn over the rest of the brill.

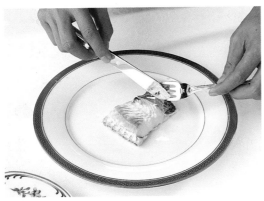

5 Remove the black skin as you did in step 2.

6 Remove the outer edge of the backbone using the spoon and fork.

7 Remove the fillet from the backbone as in step 3. Place it with the other fillet on the individual serving plate so that the skin surfaces face upward.

PRESENTATION: Pour saffron sauce over the top. (This sauce is made from the court bouillon in which the brill was poached, and it is seasoned with saffron.)

Poached whole brill

(*Barbue pochée*)

88

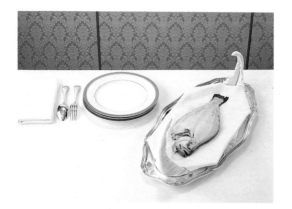

Utensils: serving spoon, fork, plate for waste

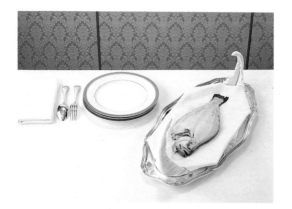

1 Place the brill so that the tail is nearest to you. Run a serving spoon along the backbone from the head to the tail.

2 Continue running the spoon around the inside of the outer edge of the backbone. Repeat with the other side.

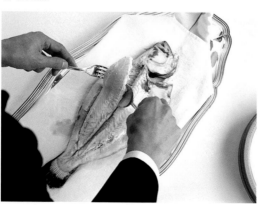

3 Insert the spoon beneath the upper meat from the central incision. Supporting with a fork, slide the spoon from the head to the tail. Remove the fillet.

4 Gently supporting the bottom of the fillet with the spoon and fork, place it on a plate. Be careful not to break the meat.

Kitchen preparation: Carefully place the brill, white skin up, on a service napkin.

* Presentation note: Serve the fillets complete with the white skin. A brill that is 12 to 16 inches (30 to 40 cm) long will serve four people. However, since the meat of each side differs in thickness, halve each fillet and combine one piece from each side to make a portion.

5 Insert the spoon beneath the other fillet from the incision at the edge. Slide it from the head to the tail, and remove the fillet.

6 Turn the dish so that the head is nearest to you. Cut the backbone at the base of the tail, and lift the backbone using the spoon.

7 When you reach the head, hold the backbone between the spoon and fork and snap it off.

8 Turn the dish again, and remove the outer edge of the backbone. Repeat with the other edge.

9 Slide the spoon between the meat and the skin from the center of the brill. Remove the fillets and place on the plate.

PRESENTATION: Halve each fillet. Arrange the head and tail regions and two fillet pieces, one from each side, to make two complete but mixed fillets.*

Grilled seabream with marinière sauce

(Daurade grillée, sauce marinière)

Utensils: dish warmer, fish knife, serving spoon, fork, cutting plate, plate for waste

1 Lift the fish while holding it from the bottom with the serving spoon and fork. Place it on a plate so that the tail is nearest to you.

2 Cut off the head with a fish knife.

3 Make a small incision in each side with the tip of the knife.

4 Insert the spoon from the top and the fork from the belly of the fish. Slide them over the backbone toward the tail, and remove the upper meat.

* **Marinière sauce**: Sauté in olive oil a purée of red and yellow peppers, together with shallots, zucchinis, and onions; add butter.

5   Insert the spoon underneath the backbone. Slide the spoon to lift the backbone.

6   When you reach the base of the tail, remove the backbone and the tail from the lower meat.

7   Remove the belly and the rib bones using the spoon.

8   Remove all the bones from the edge.

PRESENTATION: Halve both fillets on the serving plate and place one piece so that you can see the grilled surface. Garnish with marinière sauce* and vegetables au gratin.

Roast seabream
(*Daurade rôtie*)

92

Utensils: dish warmer, fish knife, serving spoon, fork, cutting plate, plate for waste

1 Place the fish so that the tail is nearest to you. Supporting it with the flat of a fork, make an incision along the top with a fish knife.

2 Insert the tip of the fish knife into the belly as well. Run the knife along the backbone from the head to the tail.

3 Run the knife around the head. Halve the upper meat.

4 Take out each upper fillet using the serving spoon and fork.

* **Presentation note:** A large fish is best cut into four fillets. However, as the upper fillet is different in size from the lower fillet, halve each quarter fillet again and combine one of each section for each portion so as to serve each guest equally. At the time of presentation, place one piece on the plate so that the grilled surface faces up.

5 Halve the lower meat, and remove each half.

6 Cut off the tail, and turn the fish so that the head is nearest to you. Begin lifting the backbone, and remove with the head.

7 Remove the other edge of the backbone with the fish knife.

8 Remove the belly and the rib bones.

9 Cut the meat of the other side into two fillets. Halve each fillet again.

PRESENTATION: Arrange the head and tail regions and two fillet pieces from opposite sides to make two complete but mixed fillets.*

Cold salmon

(Saumon froid)

Utensils: fish-filleting knife, serving spoon, fork, plate for waste

1 From the belly side, slide the knife between the upper meat and the backbone to detach both. Cut the meat obliquely.

2 Repeat step 1 for the top side. Cut the meat lengthwise into four pieces.

3 Remove the pieces by holding them between the fish-filleting knife and the flat of the fork. Place them on a plate one after another.

4 After removing all the meat up to the incision, make another oblique incision on the belly side.

Note: Here we are cutting all the upper meat; when fewer portions are required, cut off only the quantity needed.

5 Make an incision the same way on the top side. Cut the meat lengthwise into six pieces.

6 Remove the pieces as in step 3, and place them on a plate. The bottom meat is to be sliced and removed in the same way after step 9.

7 After you have cut all the upper meat in the same way, cut off the tail with a spoon.

8 Lift the backbone with the spoon. When you reach the halfway point, snap off half of the backbone, supporting it with the fork.

9 Continue lifting the rest of the bone, and snap it off from the base of the head.

PRESENTATION: After cutting all the upper meat, place about three pieces on a plate for one serving. Serve with a mayonnaise sauce.

Grilled chicken with diable sauce

(Poulet grillé, sauce diable)

Utensils: dish warmer, carving board, boning knife, serving spoon, fork

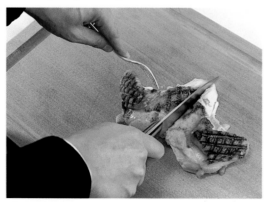

1 Place the chicken on a carving board with the legs facing you. Slightly lift the thigh with a fork, and cut off the leg using a boning knife.

2 Cut at the knee joint of the leg, separating the thigh from the drumstick.

3 Place the chicken so that the wings face you. Halve the chicken by cutting through the center of the breast meat.

4 Hold the wing with the inner curve of the fork, and cut it off at the joint.

Kitchen preparation: Make an incision along the backbone, remove the backbone, and then grill the chicken. The breastbone is removed during carving.

* **Diable sauce:** Boiling together white wine, wine vinegar, finely chopped shallots, tomatoes (or tomato paste), and peppercorns; add veal stock. Season with cayenne pepper.

5 Turn the breast meat over, and remove the breast-bone.

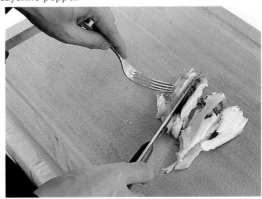

6 Slice the breast meat.

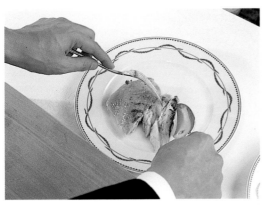

7 Place an appropriate amount of breast meat and leg meat together on the plate.

PRESENTATION: Garnish with deep-fried potatoes, bacon, mushrooms, a cherry tomato, and watercress. Pour diable sauce* over the top.

Roast chicken
(*Poulet rôti*)

Utensils: dish warmer, carving board, boning knife, serving spoon, fork

The first method, in which the chicken is cut into five pieces, allows you to serve assorted meats of different quality, such as breast meat and the leg. The second method, however, is easier.

One chicken provides four servings.

FIRST METHOD

1 Remove the paper decoration from the base of the chicken leg.

2 Transfer the watercress garnish from the plate on the dish warmer to another plate.

3 Lift the chicken with the serving spoon and fork, drain the juices from the cavity, and place the chicken on the carving board.

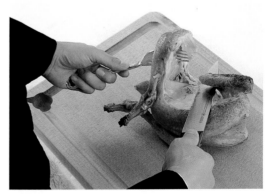

4 Place the chicken as shown. Pierce the thigh with the fork, and with the boning knife, make an incision around the leg through the skin only. Remove the leg.

Kitchen preparation: Remove the wishbone before roasting. After the chicken is roasted, drain any juices out of the cavity to avoid carving and serving difficulties.

5 Cut off the base of the leg at the joint.

6 Cut through the knee joint, separating the thigh from the drumstick. Repeat steps 4 through 6 for the other leg.

7 Place the chicken so that the breast faces upward and the head faces toward you. Cut ½ inch (1.5 cm) down from the breastbone on the right side.

8 Bring the blade down along the breastbone through the wing joint, and remove the breast meat together with the wing.

9 Cut off the end of the wing. Repeat steps 7 and 8 for the left side of the breastbone, and cut off the end of that wing as well.

10 Lay the chicken flat. Pierce the fork deep into the carcass in order to keep it steady. Insert the knife between the white meat and the bone.

11 Hold the white meat down with the knife. Using the fork, lift the bone to remove the white meat from it.

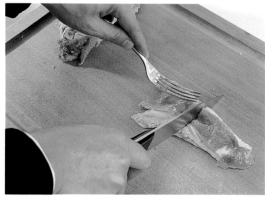

12 Halve the white meat removed in step 11.

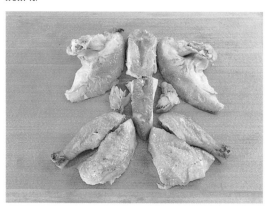

13 Carve the chicken into five pieces. The white meat and legs are cut in half. Remove the oysters.

SECOND METHOD

PRESENTATION: Garnish with sautéed mushrooms, watercress, potato, carrot, and zucchini. Top with a sauce made from the reserved juices, wine, and stock.

7 After removing the legs, place the chicken with the breast facing upward and the head facing you. Pierce the carcass with the fork to keep it steady.

8 Cut slightly down from the breastbone on the right side. Cut through the wing joint to remove the breast meat with the white meat.

9   Cut off the end of the wing using the fork for support.

10   Repeat step 8 for the left side of the breastbone.

11   Cut off the end of the wing.

12   Cut off the meat at the upper part of the breast.

13   Remove the "oysters" with a spoon.

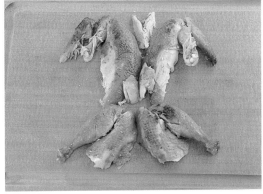

14   Carve the chicken into four pieces: two breast meat, which are attached to the white meat, and two legs, which are cut into halves.

Duck à l'orange

(Canard à l'orange)

Utensils: dish warmer, carving board, fish-filleting knife, chef's knife, serving spoon, fork

FIRST METHOD

1 Remove the orange peel and move the watercress to another plate. Drain the juices out of the cavity.

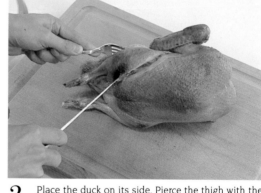

2 Place the duck on its side. Pierce the thigh with the fork, and make an incision around the leg through the skin only.

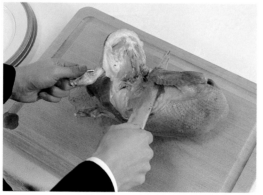

3 Supporting the duck with the chef's knife, pull the leg up with the fork. Using the chef's knife, cut the joint to remove the leg completely.

4 Turn the duck over so that the back faces you. Remove the other leg following steps 2 and 3.

Kitchen preparation: Remove the wishbone of the duck before roasting. After the duck is roasted, drain any juices out of the cavity. One duck provides two servings.

Note: At the time the breast meat is served, the leg is not completely cooked. If the guest requests the leg, remove the leg from the carcass and put it back in the oven to cook through to the inside.

5 Turn the duck slightly on an angle, with the breast facing up and the head facing you. Cut along the breastbone on the right side.

6 Using the fork, pierce deeply into where the leg was removed. Supporting the duck firmly, begin slicing the breast meat with a fish-filleting knife.

7 Move the fish-filleting knife from the head to the tail to make a slice.

8 Continue this slicing method until you reach the breastbone.

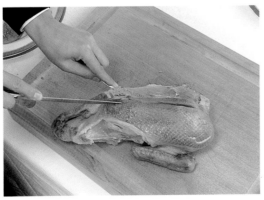

9 Turn the duck so that the breast faces up and the tail faces you. Supporting the duck with the fork, make an incision along the breastbone on the other side.

10 Move the fish-filleting knife from the head to the tail, slicing the breast meat as you did in steps 7 and 8.

* **Sweet and sour orange sauce:** Boil water with sugar until it turns a caramel color; add orange juice and stock.

2   Place the duck breast up with the head toward you. Using the chef's knife, make an incision in the center of the breast along the breastbone.

3   Supporting the duck with a fork, make an incision around the leg.

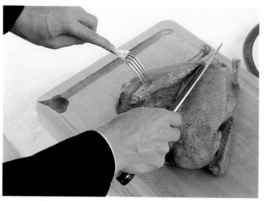

4   Insert the chef's knife into the central incision. Remove only the breast meat, by lifting it out with a fork.

5   Slice the breast meat.

PRESENTATION: Sprinkle with orange peel. Garnish with the flesh of the orange, potatoes Anna, and watercress. Top with orange sauce.*

Roast pigeon
(*Pigeon rôti*)

Utensils: dish warmer, carving board, boning knife, serving spoon, fork

1 Place the pigeon breast up with the head toward you. Cut with a boning knife slightly down the central breastbone on the right or left side.

2 Completely halve the pigeon, and remove the central breastbone and the backbone completely from the meat.

3 Remove any breastbone left by supporting it with the knife and pulling up with the fork to separate the bone and meat.

PRESENTATION: Place the pigeon on potatoes Annet. Garnish with puréed chestnuts, carrots, green peas, and watercress. Top with a sauce made from the reserved juices, wine, and stock.

Roast turkey

(*Dinde rôtie*)

Utensils: carving board, chef's knife, fish-filleting knife, serving spoon, fork

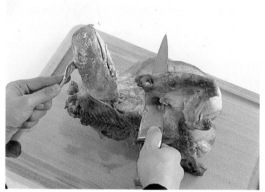

1 Place the turkey so that the back faces you. Cut around the leg with the chef's knife, and use the fork to remove the leg by pulling.

2 Cut the knee joint, separating the thigh from the drumstick.

3 Run the chef's knife parallel to the bone in order to slice the thigh.

4 Slice all the thigh meat.

5 Place the turkey so that the breast faces up and the leg end faces you. Slice off a small portion of the breast skin using the fish-filleting knife.

6 To properly slice the breast meat, move the fish-filleting knife from the head to the top of the breast.

7 Support the turkey with the fork, and slice the breast meat as wide as possible along the curve of the breast.

8 Slice all the meat on one side of the breast.

PRESENTATION: Garnish with watercress, sautéed potatoes and mushrooms. Top with a sauce made from the reserved vegetable and turkey juices, wine, and stock.

Roast leg of lamb

(Gigot d'agneau rôti)

Utensils: dish warmer, carving board, leg holder, boning knife, carving knife, serving spoon, fork

1 Put the end of the shank bone into the leg holder and tighten the screw to fix firmly.

2 Place the leg so that the bulk of the meat (which is called *noix*) faces down. Cut off the gristle over the shank bone with a carving knife.

3 Turn the leg over so that the *noix* faces up. Cut off the small piece of meat (knuckle) located at the back of the knee joint.

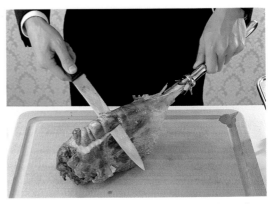

4 Again turn the leg over so that the *noix* faces down. Begin carving the outside of the leg (*sous-noix*), where there is less meat.

5 Holding the leg firmly, insert the carving knife parallel to the leg bone. Cut a thin slice.

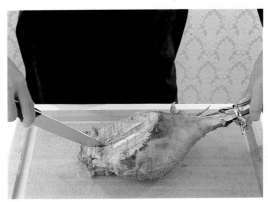

6 If the leg bone becomes visible, make an incision on either side along the bone using the boning knife so that it will be easier to carve the *noix* in the next step.

7 Turn the leg over so that the *noix* faces up. Holding the leg firmly, insert the carving knife vertically to the bone.

8 Move the carving knife along the bone, and cut slices as wide as possible.

9 After slicing the *noix*, remove the rest of the meat from the bone using the boning knife. Cut it into pieces. Cut the knuckle into the proper size.

PRESENTATION: Arrange the *noix*, the *sous-noix*, and the knuckle on the plate. Garnish with potato and garlic croquettes and watercress.

Pepper steak with Madeira sauce

(Steak au poivre, sauce madère)

118

Utensils: dish warmer, plate, soup bowl, dinner knife, serving spoon, fork

Ingredients (2 servings): 2 pepper steaks; ⅜ (150 cc) Madeira sauce (see p. 109); 2t. (10 g) butter; brandy; salt

1 Preheat the pan, and remove from heat. Pour brandy over the meat.

2 Ignite.

3 Use the serving spoon and fork to remove the meat from the pan. Place it on a plate.

4 Invert a soup bowl over the meat to keep it warm.

Kitchen preparation: Cook meat as the guest prefers, and place it in another pan for service. Add a small quantity of butter, and keep warm.

5 Pour Madeira sauce into the cooking pan.

6 Use the spoon to scrape the bottom of the pan, deglazing the pan juices.

7 Add butter to the sauce and melt, stirring slowly.

8 If necessary, season with salt.

9 Place the meat on the side of the plate using the spoon and fork.

PRESENTATION: Garnish with sautéed potatoes, braised endive, and watercress. Pour sauce over the steak.

Veal kidney in port wine sauce

(Rognon de veau au porto)

Utensils: dish warmer, cutting plate, soup bowl, paring knife, serving spoon, fork

Ingredients (4 servings): 2 veal kidneys; ½ cup (250 cc) port wine sauce*; 2 T. (50 cc) fresh cream; 2 T. (30 g) butter; 2 T. (50 cc) port wine; brandy; salt; pepper

1 Preheat the pan containing the kidneys, and remove it from the heat. Pour brandy over the kidneys.

2 Ignite.

3 Place the kidneys on a plate, and invert a soup bowl over them to keep them warm.

4 Pour port into the cooking pan. Deglaze the pan juices, and boil them down for a moment.

Kitchen preparation: Remove any fat from around the kidney and muscles. Roast the kidneys until the inside is medium done. Place them in another pan for serving, add a small amount of butter, and keep warm. Be careful not to overcook the kidneys, as they will become tough.

* **Port wine sauce:** Sauté morels and finely chopped shallots together in butter. Add port, boil, and add veal stock. Add fresh cream and butter in the presence of the guests.

5 Gently supporting the kidney with a serving fork, use the paring knife to cut it into slices ⅛ inch (5 mm) thick.

6 Pour the sauce with morels into the cooking pan.

7 Add fresh cream, and mix together.

8 Add butter and melt, stirring slowly.

9 Return the sliced kidneys to the pan to rewarm.

PRESENTATION: Garnish with fettuccine mixed with sautéed mushrooms. Pour port wine sauce* over the top.

Steak tartare
(*Steak tartare*)

Utensils: soup bowl, serving spoon, fork

Ingredients (1 serving): 4 oz. (120 g) lean meat of beef (rump); 1 egg yolk; 1 T. (15 g) onion; 1 T. (15 g) pickled cucumber; 1 t. (5 g) anchovy; 2 t. (10 g) parsley; pinch of capers; pinch of garlic; ½ t. (3 g) mustard; 1 T. (25 cc) salad oil; 1 t. (8 cc) ketchup; small amounts of Worcestershire sauce, Tabasco, and paprika; salt; pepper

1   Place the yolk in a soup bowl, and add mustard.

2   Using a serving spoon, slowly blend salad oil into the mixture to thicken it.

3   Mix in the ketchup.

4   Add finely chopped onion.

Kitchen preparation: Chop the lean beef (rump) into small pieces with the chef's knife. Form into a mound, make a hole in the center, and place the yolk in it. Finely chop the onion, pickled cucumber, anchovy, parsley, capers, and garlic.

5   Add pickled cucumber, garlic, capers, and anchovy.

6   Add parsley, and mix together with the spoon.

7   Add Tabasco, Worcestershire sauce, and paprika.

8   Add beef.

9   Season with salt and pepper. Form into a round shape using the spoon and fork.

PRESENTATION: Place directly on a plate.

Avocado stuffed with crayfish

(*Avocat aux écrevisses*)

Utensils: soup bowls, teaspoon, paring knife, serving spoon, 2 forks

Ingredients: 1 avocado; 12 crayfish; shredded lettuce

Prepare cocktail sauce using 3 T. (80 cc) mayonnaise; 1 T. (25 cc) ketchup; small amounts of Worcestershire sauce and brandy; half a lemon; Tabasco; paprika; salt; pepper

1 Place the mayonnaise in a soup bowl.

2 Pierce the lemon half with a fork, and squeeze a small amount of juice into the mayonnaise.

3 Add ketchup.

4 Add Worcestershire sauce, Tabasco, and paprika. Mix together.

Kitchen preparation: Remove the intestine from along the back of the crayfish, boil the crayfish with salt, and remove its shell.

5 Finish preparing the cocktail sauce by pouring in the brandy and seasoning with salt and pepper.

6 Place the crayfish in another soup bowl, and add some of the cocktail sauce.

7 Mix them together. Add more sauce as necessary.

8 Using the paring knife, make a deep incision lengthwise around the avocado. The blade should touch the pit.

9 Twist each half of the avocado in a different direction in order to separate the halves. Stick the blade of the knife into the pit to remove it.

10 Squeeze the lemon juice over the flesh of the avocado.

11 Scoop out the flesh of the avocado with a tea-spoon. Add it to the crayfish cocktail sauce.

12 Mix well with the serving spoon and fork.

13 Fill the avocado cup with the crayfish mixture.

14 Place the avocado cup on the shredded lettuce, which is on the plate.

PRESENTATION: Serve this dish along with a finger bowl.

Spaghetti with shellfish
(*Spaghetti aux fruits de mer*)

Utensils: dish warmer, sauté pan, serving spoon, fork

Ingredients (2 servings): 5 oz. (140 g) spaghetti

Prepare sauce using 6 shrimp; 1.8 oz (50 g) cuttlefish; 10 small clams; 10 mussels; ½ T. (8 g) garlic; half a chili pepper; 1 ½ (40 cc) olive oil; 4 T. (100 cc) tomato sauce; 1 ⅓ (30 cc) clam stock; parsley; salt; pepper

1 Heat olive oil in the sauté pan.

2 Place finely chopped garlic and chili pepper into the pan. Sauté until golden brown. Do not scorch.

3 Add clams and shrimp.

4 Add cuttlefish and mussels.

Apple
(*Pomme*)

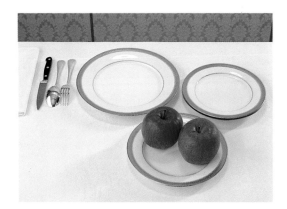

Utensils: paring knife, serving spoon, fork, cutting plate, plate for waste

1 Hollow out the stem using the tip of the paring knife, and place on a plate.

2 Repeat step 1 for the other end.

3 Cut a slice off the bottom of the apple to make it steady.

4 Stick the fork firmly into the hollow from which the stem was removed.

5 Pare the apple using the paring knife. Work from the bottom to the top, toward the fork.

5 You can also pare the apple spirally, rotating it with the fork.

6 Insert the blade of the knife between the tines of the fork, and cut the apple in half.

7 Stick the fork into the core to keep it steady, and cut around the core with the knife.

8 Remove the core.

PRESENTATION: Serve the halves of the apple together with the stem as they originally were, or cut the apple into four pieces.

Pineapple
(*Ananas*)

134

Utensils for preparation: carving board, paring knife, ham-slicing knife, serving spoon, fork, and plate for waste

FIRST METHOD (serving the whole pineapple)

1 Cut a thin slice off the bottom of the pineapple with the ham-slicing knife.

2 Hold the top leaves, and rest the pineapple on the cut base. Run the knife from the top toward the bottom to cut away the peel.

3 To remove the eyes, make an incision spirally around the pineapple using the tip of the paring knife.

4 Stick the tip of the paring knife into the eye portion. Remove it by pulling gently.

5 Lay the pineapple on its side, and make a deep incision around the core with the paring knife.

6 Make slices using the ham-slicing knife.

7 Remove the core with the fork.

SECOND METHOD (serving a portion of the pineapple)

PRESENTATION: Arrange the slices of pineapple on the plate, and place the top portion in the center. Serve with a sugar bowl, and top with kirsch.

1 Cut off the top of the pineapple about 2 inches (5 cm) from the root of the leaves. This top portion will be used as an ornament at the time of service.

2 Lay the pineapple lengthwise on the carving board. Rotating it with your left hand, move the ham-slicing knife in a slicing motion in order to cut off the peel.

136

3 Assume that you will serve two slices to one person, and pare as far as necessary.

4 Cut slices of the pineapple.

5 Cut off the eyes from around the flesh using the paring knife.

6 Using the serving fork for support, cut out the core.

PRESENTATION: Place the slices on a plate. Replace the top portion of the pineapple on the bottom portion.

Crêpes Suzette
(*Crêpes Suzette*)

Utensils: dish warmer, sauté pan, serving spoon, fork

Ingredients (2 servings): 4 crêpes; 2 T. (30 g) granulated sugar; 1 ½ T. (20 g) butter; ¼ cup (100 cc) orange juice; squeeze of lemon; Grand Marnier; brandy; orange sections; orange peel (thinly stripped and briefly boiled)

FIRST METHOD (with flambé)

1 Pour granulated sugar into the heated sauté pan, and cook until it turns caramel in color.

2 Add butter and dissolve into the caramel.

3 Mix in the orange juice.

4 Add a little lemon juice.

138

5 Boil together for a moment.

6 Pour in Grand Marnier.

7 Holding the crêpe with the tines of the fork, lift up the crêpe and rotate so that the crêpe wraps around the fork.

8 Unroll the crêpe, and place it in the sauté pan.

9 Soak the crêpe with the sauce. Fold it in half, being careful not to tear it.

10 Fold the crêpe in half again, and move it to the side of the pan.

11 Repeat steps 7 through 10 for each of the four crêpes.

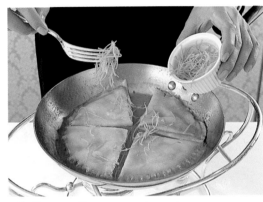

12 Sprinkle orange peel over the top.

13 Place the orange sections onto the crêpes.

14 Pour brandy over the top.

15 Flambé.

PRESENTATION: Place the crêpes on the plate. Place the peel and orange sections on top of the crêpes, and top with the sauce.

* **Suzette butter:** Grate the orange and lemon peels, and squeeze the juice from the orange. Add granulated sugar to butter. Mix well with a whisk until it turns whitish. Mix in orange juice. Add the orange peel, lemon peel, Grand Marnier, and brandy. Beat firmly with the whisk until soft and smooth.

SECOND METHOD (without flambé)

140

Utensils: dish warmer, sauté pan, serving spoon, fork

Ingredients (2 servings): 4 crêpes

Prepare 5T. (75g) Suzette butter* using ⅞ cup (200 g) soft butter; 1 T. (30 cc) Grand Marnier; 1 T. (30 cc) brandy; ¼ cup (60 g) granulated sugar; 1 orange; ½ lemon

1 Preheat the pan, and melt 2 tablespoons of Suzette butter in it.

2 Holding the crêpe with the tines of the fork, lift up the crêpe and rotate it so that the crêpe wraps around the fork.

3 Unroll the crêpe, and place it in the frying pan.

4 Spread the melted butter over the surface of the crêpe, and fold the crêpe in half.

5 Fold the crêpe in half again, and move it to the side of the pan.

6 Add 1 tablespoon of Suzette butter.

7 Place a second crêpe in the pan as you did in steps 2 and 3.

8 Repeat steps 4 through 7 for each of the four crêpes. Cook them for a moment.

9 Place the crêpes on the plate, and top with the butter left in the pan.

Peach flambé

(*Pêches flambées*)

142

Utensils: dish warmer, sauté pan, serving spoon, fork

Ingredients (3 servings): 6 peaches (canned, halved lengthwise); ½ lemon; 2 T. (30 g) granulated sugar; ¼ cup (100 cc) syrup from the canned peaches; Cointreau; vanilla ice cream

1 Preheat the pan. Add granulated sugar.

2 Pierce the lemon with a fork, and squeeze the juice over the sugar.

3 When it turns caramel in color, place the peaches in the pan.

4 Pour in peach syrup. Let it dissolve into the caramel.

5 Boil down the syrup and spoon it over the peaches.

6 Remove from the heat, and add Cointreau.

7 Flambé.

PRESENTATION: Place the peaches on vanilla ice cream, and top with the sauce. (You may use different flavors of ice cream and top with almonds as well.)

Banana flambé
(*Bananes flambées*)

Utensils: dish warmer, sauté pan, serving spoon, fork

Ingredients (2 servings): 6 banana halves (halved lengthwise); 1 ½ T. (20 g) butter; 2 T. (30 g) granulated sugar; 2 t. (10 g) brown sugar; rum; sliced toasted almonds

1   Preheat the pan. Melt butter.

2   Add the granulated sugar.

3   Add the brown sugar.

4   Mix the butter and sugar. Heat until it turns caramel in color.

5 Place the banana in a line along the bottom of the pan so that the insides face up. Cook until brown.

6 When the surface turns brown, turn the banana over using the serving spoon and fork.

7 Brown the other side. Pour rum over top.

8 Flambé.

9 Place the banana onto the plate flat side down, and top with the sauce.

PRESENTATION: Top with sliced almonds.

Cheese

"Dessert without cheese is like a pretty girl without one eye"—so said the French gourmet Brillat Savarin, who wrote *The Physiology of Taste*. As he says, cheese is an essential food in Western, especially French, cuisine. In France, it is eaten before sweet desserts at a meal. It goes well with wine and bread and is also nutritious.

French cheeses are divided into several types according to the method of production, degree of ripeness, firmness, and other characteristics.

Types of Cheese

In this section we will look at some typical cheeses that are classified according to their firmness.

Fresh soft cheese (Fromage blanc, Petit-Suisse, Boursault, and ricotta). These cheeses are neither ripened nor dehydrated very much in the manufacturing process. They cannot be kept for a long time and so should be eaten soon after they are produced. They have a mild and light taste.

Soft cheese The curds of soft cheese are drained naturally and ripened for a short time only. Three kinds of cheese are included in this category:

- White molded cheese—*Camembert*, *Brie*, and *Saint-Marcellin*. The rind is covered with white mold and is goldish white in color. The interior is creamy and easy to spread.

- Washed-rind cheese—*Pont-l'Évêque*, *Munster*, *Livarot*, and *Maroilles*. These cheeses are bathed in salt water. The surface is orange and shiny, and it is moist to the touch. These cheeses have a strong, invigorating smell.

- Goat cheese—*Banon*, *Crottin de Chavignol*, *Sainte-Maure* (some are covered with ashes), and *Pyramide*. This cheese is made from goat's milk.

Semihard cheese (*Cantal*, *Saint-Nectaire*, *Tomme de Savoie*, *Reblochon*) In making, semihard cheeses, the curds are cooked in the whey, pressed, and aged.

- Blue cheese—*Roquefort* (made from goat's milk), *Bleu de Bresse*, and *Fourme d'Ambert*. Cheeses marbled throughout with veins of blue or green molds.

Hard cheese (*Beaufort*, *Emmental*, *Gruyère*, and *Parmesan*) The curds of hard cheeses are cooked in the whey (after coagulation, the temperature of the whey is raised above the coagulating temperature) and pressed. The cheeses are ripened for a long time and have a mild and sweet taste.

Processed cheese (*Fromage aux fines herbes* or spiced cheese) This type of cheese is made by heating, melting, and sterilizing natural cheeses. This process kills the microorganisms of natural cheese, which results in the cheese losing some of its flavor. Therefore, other ingredients, including spices, are often blended with the cheese. Processed cheese keeps well and is also less expensive than natural cheese.

Serving and Keeping Cheese

Cheese should be removed from the refrigerator at least 1 hour before serving so that it may warm to room temperature. It should be covered with a moist cloth to prevent drying out.

At the time of presentation to guests, various kinds of cheese are arranged on a cheese tray, which is placed on a cart (see photo on page 146). Soft or soft spreadable cheese, such as Camembert, is better placed on an earthenware tray (there is a tray that has a removable glass plate for easy washing after use). Cheese with a dry rind is best placed on a wooden tray (such as olive, oak, or walnut). Metal trays should not be used for serving cheese. If there is a cheese with a strong smell, prepare another tray for it so the other cheeses do not absorb its odor. Always remember to use a clean tray. When preparing your tray, choose cheeses that are popular with guests. Avoid cheeses with peculiar flavors or tastes. Choose one or two kinds of cheese from each category mentioned earlier.

After the guests have made their selections, the cheeses should be cut so that every guest is served an equal portion. To maintain freshness, keep the cut section to a minimum, so the inside of the cheese comes in minimal contact with the air. (This is especially important with spreadable cheese, as this method reduces the spreading of the interior of the cheese.) There are specific ways of cutting the various kinds, sizes, and shapes of cheese, ways of cutting various kinds, sizes and shapes of cheese.

Round cheese

- Average-sized cheese is cut radially from the center into four to eight equal sections.

- Large-sized cheese is sliced radially. In the case of a very large and thick cheese such as *Roquefort*, each slice is cut again into sections.

- Small-sized cheese is cut into halves.

Brie

① Livarot; ② Banon; ③ Boursault; ④ Crottin de Chavignol; and ⑤ Saint-Marcellin

Cylindrical cheese

- It is usually cut into circular slices.
- Large-sized cheese is cut into circular slices and then divided equally into the proper sizes.

Square or rectangular cheese

- Square-shaped cheese is usually cut radially from the center into four or eight equal pieces.
- Pyramid-shaped cheese is cut radially from the center as well.
- Large and thick cheese (such as *Emmental*) is thinly sliced and cut equally into the proper sizes.

If possible, each type of cheese should be cut with a different knife. The knives should be sharp, of course, so that the cut section will be uniform and straight.

The rest of the cheese should be rewrapped and stored in a cool place at about 47°F (8°C) with proper humidity. Each individual cheese, not only cheese with a strong smell, should be wrapped separately from other cheese to avoid mingling flavors.

Since cheese is a very delicate food, it should be served at the right point in its maturation. Cheese generally is sold when it is ready to eat, so it is best to serve it soon after purchasing it.

Roquefort

149

① Reblochon; ② Pyramide; ③ Camembert; and ④ Maroilles

① Emmental; ② Fourme d'Ambert; and ③ Sainte-Maure

6

Wine Service

The Sommelier, or Wine Waiter

As discussed earlier, the restaurant's service staff—that is, the *maître d'hôtel* or captain, head waiter, and waiter—is in charge of serving meals. In a large restaurant, there is also a *sommelier* or wine waiter who is in charge of all wine service. Since wine is an integral part of Western cuisine and wine choice can add to or detract from the meal, the *sommelier* plays an important role in the restaurant, equal to that of the *maître d'hôtel*.

The Work Apparel

You can distinguish a *sommelier* from other service staff, as he is dressed differently. His apparel is a manifestation of the tradition and significance of the job of the *sommelier* (see photo on page 17).

- Clothes—He wears a black suit jacket and trousers and a white shirt with a black bow tie.
- Apron—A *sommelier* was originally the highest-ranking among workers in the wine cellar and as such was chosen to serve wine to guests in the dining room. As a vestige of that role, he wears an apron inside his jacket.
- *Taste-vin*, or wine-tasting cup—Originally, this utensil was used for wine tasting (see page 164), but it is now seldom used.
- Pin with a design of a bunch of grapes—This symbol of the *sommelier* is worn on the left lapel of the jacket.

The *sommelier* always carries these two things with him:

- Waiter's corkscrew (see page 162)—This folding utensil contains a knife used to cut off the foil covering the neck of the wine bottle and a corkscrew for drawing the cork out.
- Service napkin.

Daily Work

A *sommelier* must serve the wines that best complement each dish. To achieve this objective, the *sommelier* must be knowledgeable regarding the purchasing, storage, and selling of wines, which are his daily duties.

Buying Wine   To select wines of fine quality that have the ideal regional characteristics, a knowledge of wine tasting, wines, and their regions is essential. Upon purchasing the wine, the *sommelier* should record in the cellar log book the appellation, the vintage, the year and date of purchase, the quantity of wine purchased, and any other pertinent information. When purchasing wine, the *sommelier* must take into account the kinds and quantities being stored in the wine cellar at that time and the usual demand at the restaurant.

Storing Wine   It is often said that wine is a living substance. As such, it must be stored with great care in the wine cellar so that it can be served at its best and its original characteristics can be enjoyed to the fullest.

Selling Wine   Selling the wine, which is the most important task of the *sommelier*, means selecting and serving the wine that is most suitable for the dishes ordered by the guests. This means that the *sommelier* must not only have a mastery of the techniques necessary for serving wine, he must also be extremely knowledgeable about various dishes, desserts, cheeses, and the ingredients of each.

Serving Wine in the Dining Room

In the dining room, the *sommelier* mainly serves wine, including apéritifs and digestifs.

Apéritifs   Apéritifs should be served to the guests about the time that the menu is presented. Because apéritifs are for the stimulation of one's appetite, it is best to avoid a drink with a high alcohol content. A dry or slightly bitter drink is quite suitable. Examples include dry sherry, Campari, kir (a mix of crème de cassis and white Burgundy), kir royal (a mix of crème de cassis and Champagne), and chilled white wine.

Wine   After the food orders are taken, the *sommelier* presents the menu to the guests. If the guest cannot decide which wine to choose, the *sommelier* can then suggest a suitable wine for the food ordered and its price. At this time, the *sommelier* must infer from the conversation with the guests whether they are ready to order a wine regardless of how much it costs or whether he must literally "sell" the wines.

Digestifs (cordials or liqueurs)   Digestifs are served to aid digestion and to complement the fine aftertaste of the meal. Digestifs are ordered after the guests have finished their coffee. Examples include brandy, spirits, and sweet liqueurs such as Grand Marnier, kirsch, mirabelle, and poire Williams.

Wine and Food Combinations

Wine and the Main Course

Combinations of wine and food are infinite because there is such a variety of both. The guest decides on a wine according to his or her taste and budget. However, the *sommelier* is often asked to suggest a wine that "improves the dish." These rules can help:

- In the case of a dish seasoned with wine, choose the same wine for drinking.
- In the case of regional cuisine, choose a wine from the same region.
- The wine and the food should match in intensity of flavor.

The same dish may have a different flavor at different restaurants because of subtle variations in seasonings, the thickness of sauces, and the ingredients. Therefore, the *sommelier* must be well aware of the smell and taste of each dish in his restaurant. He must choose a wine that does not spoil the flavor of the food or overpower it, but that matches the intensity of the food's flavor. (This harmony in flavor must also be considered when combining wine with cheese or dessert.)

Although selling wine is one of the most significant jobs of a *sommelier*, he should not suggest too many wines for one meal. A wine that suits the main dish should be suggested. If necessary, a second wine that suits the other dishes may also be suggested. When numerous varieties of wines are to be suggested throughout a meal, the following rules apply:

- Serve an acidic wine before a mild wine.
- Serve a wine that has low tannin content before one with a high tannin content. Tannin is more prevalent in red wine than in white. Tannin comes from grape stems and skins and has an astringent, puckerish quality when the wine is young. As the wine matures, the tannic quality lessens and the wine develops a smoother, rounder taste.
- Serve a young wine before a long-matured wine.
- Serve a light wine before a robust wine.

Wine and Cheese

When eating cheese with a meal, guests often choose to drink the same wine that was served with the previous dishes. However, this does not allow guests to enjoy the cheese to the fullest.

Within each region of France and other countries, wine and cheese are produced in many different varieties, so the combinations are more numerous than those of food and wine. The rules regarding wine selection for cheese are the same as the rules for wine and food combination:

- In the case of a regional cheese, choose a wine from the same region.

- The wine and the cheese should match in intensity of flavor. Furthermore, it has generally been said that red wine is most suitable for cheese; white wine, however, is also suitable, except with hard cheeses. Hard cheese has a far more balanced flavor than others because of its longer ripening period, and red wine with a good balance between tannin and acidity is a good match for such cheeses.

Since every type of cheese has its own characteristics (such as fat content and the degree of ripening), the following additional rules can serve as a guide for the *sommelier*:

- A light and acidic dry white wine is also suitable with soft goat cheese.

- Normandy Camembert, which is typical of French soft cheese, goes nicely with cider from the same region, rather than wine.

- For blue cheese, a kind of semihard cheese, a sweet and mild white wine or a full-bodied red wine is best.

In France the relationship between wine and cheese is so important that they say, "It is cheese that brings out the flavor of a great wine to the fullest and erases the faults of an inferior quality wine." It is the job of a *sommelier* to enable guests to appreciate to the fullest not only the greatness of the wines but also the rich flavor of the cheese—an experience that reinforces the pleasures of the whole meal.

Wine and Dessert

The wine and the dessert should also match in intensity of flavor. Generally a sweet wine such as Sauternes, which is just as sweet as a dessert, matches a dessert well. Champagne is the only wine that can be an apéritif and can also be matched to any dish; it is often preferred with dessert. However, it is best to avoid brut, which contains almost no sugar and is too dissimilar to the mellowness of a dessert.

How to Preserve the Quality of the Wine

Wine Storage

After the *sommelier* confirms that the wine has ideal regional characteristics and quality, he then purchases the wine by considering its price and the demand for it in the restaurant. Until the time of serving, the wine must be stored correctly in the wine cellar in order to preserve the quality of the wine and promote further moderate maturation. At this time it should be kept in mind that wine is a living substance and is very sensitive to any stimulus. The following conditions must therefore be maintained in the wine cellar.

Temperature In the wine cellar the temperature must remain fixed year round. The standard temperature is a bit lower than room temperature, about 10°C to 14°C; the ideal temperature is 11°C to 12°C. If the temperature changes rapidly, the wine ages prematurely.

Light It should be almost dark in the wine cellar. Intense light such as fluorescent will go through a bottle of wine, causing it to age prematurely and to develop an unpleasant taste. Generally an underground cellar is ideal.

Humidity The wine cellar should maintain a humidity level of 65 to 70 percent. If it is too dry inside the cellar, the cork will dry. This will allow the wine to come into contact with the air, causing a deterioration in the quality of the wine. If it is too humid, the wine itself will not be affected; however, the label or the cork will become moldy. If the label becomes unreadable due to mold, the *sommelier* will not be able to identify the wine; the appearance of the label will also hinder the presentation of the wine to the guests. If it is too dry in the cellar, place a humidifier inside or water the sand that is spread on the floor of the cellar.

Vibration Since wine is a living substance, it is important to keep it free from vibration. A very slight vibration will not affect the wine, but a strong one will disturb the sediment that has settled in the bottle. Once a bottle of wine has been placed in the cellar, it is best not to move it until it is time to serve the wine to the guests.

Smell Wine easily absorbs odors; therefore, it is important that nothing but wine be kept in the wine cellar.

Laying the bottles   The cork should remain in contact with the wine inside the bottle so it does not become dry. Therefore, the bottle should always be stored horizontally.

Checking the log   It is important to review the cellar log book, in which you record the purchase date of each wine, and to serve the wine to the guests at the appropriate maturity date.

In addition to the wine cellar, restaurants often have a room called a day cellar between the wine cellar and the dining room. This room stores wines at the proper temperature and allows the *sommelier* the convenience of not having to go to the wine cellar. The wines that are ordered regularly should be restocked in the day cellar every day, and the wines that are ordered less often should be replaced once a week or so. At least one bottle of each wine mentioned on the wine list should be stored in the day cellar.

Temperature of Wine for Serving

Maintaining optimum conditions in the wine cellar is meaningless if the wine is not served properly. The temperature of the wine is very important when serving; the *sommelier* must know the ideal or most suitable temperature for each wine.

Generally it is said that white wine is to be served chilled and red wine is to be served at room temperature. However, "room temperature" originally meant the temperature of the dining room in a European palace in the eighteenth century. Today, with central heating and cooling, "room temperature" can be very vague. Generally, the ideal serving temperatures of wines are as follows:

- 68°F (20°C) for full-bodied red wines that are rich in tannin (high-quality Bordeaux, Burgundy, etc.)
- 64°F (18°C) for light red wines with less tannin
- 55°F (13°C) for full-bodied dry white wines and very sweet white wines
- 50°F (10°C) for light dry white wines, light sweet white wines, rosé wines, and Champagne

When wine has been stored at the ideal storage temperature, be careful not to spoil the flavor by chilling or warming it too rapidly to the ideal serving temperature. Use an ice bucket to chill the wine, or slowly bring the wine to room temperature.

Wine Service Techniques

How to Open and Pour a Bottle of White Wine

Carry the bottle of white wine in an ice bucket that is 90 percent filled with ice and water, and place it on the ice bucket stand. If there is no ice bucket stand, put the ice bucket on a large plate that contains a napkin, and place it on the guest's table or on a side table. When you carry the ice bucket, it looks best if you lift it securely with one hand while supporting it with the other hand.

Follow this procedure when serving white wine (see photos on page 159):

1. Before drawing the cork, present the wine to the guest to confirm that it is the wine ordered.
2. Replace the bottle in the ice bucket. Using the corkscrew knife, cut the foil covering the neck of the bottle just below the lip.
3. Strip the foil from around the lip of the bottle.
4. Wipe around the lip of the bottle with a service napkin after removing the foil.
5. Place the point of the waiter's corkscrew in the center of the cork.
6. Slowly turn the corkscrew so that it twists straight down into the cork. Continue turning until you reach the end of the cork, but be careful not to pierce it, or chips from the cork will drop into the wine.
7. Place the lever, which is at the end of the waiter's corkscrew, on the lip of the bottle.
8. Grip the neck of the bottle together with the lever and draw the cork up slowly.
9. When the cork is almost drawn, use your right hand to gently pull it out. Check the wine's quality by smelling the cork.
10. Wipe the top of the bottle again with the service napkin.
11. Take the bottle out of the ice bucket, wipe it dry with the service napkin, and hold the bottle so that the label faces up. Pour the wine into the glass slowly, being careful not to touch the glass with the bottle. The glass should not be filled more than two-thirds full. When you have finished pouring, twist the wrist slightly so that you turn the top of the bottle. By doing this you avoid any dripping. If there are any drops left on the top of the bottle after pouring, wipe them off with the service napkin. After serving all the guests, place the bottle back in the ice bucket to keep it cool.

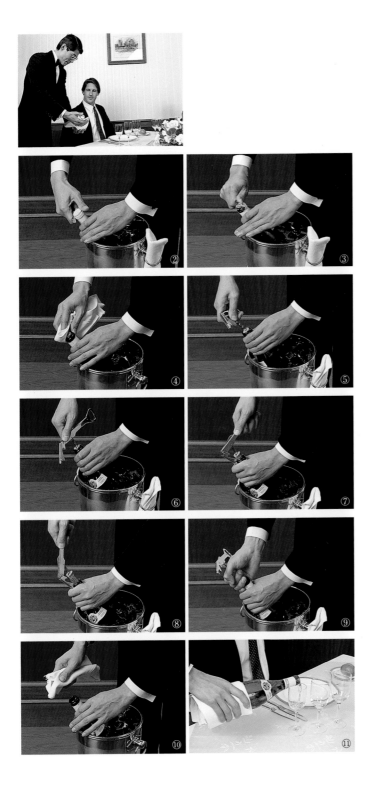

How to Open and Pour a Bottle of Red Wine

Red wine should be treated with care so as not to disturb the sediment in the bottle. A wine basket is usually used for serving red wine. If the wine basket is so shallow that wine might spill from the bottle when the cork is drawn, place a plate face down under the wine basket. Follow this procedure when serving red wine (see the photos on page 161):

(see the photos on page 161)

① Place the wine bottle in the wine basket, which contains a service napkin to avoid dripping when pouring. Present the wine to the guest, with the label facing up so the guest can confirm that it is the wine ordered.

② Using the corkscrew knife, cut the underside of the foil covering the neck of the bottle just below the lip.

③ Continue carefully cutting the foil around the neck.

④ Remove the foil top.

⑤ Wipe around the lip of the bottle with a service napkin.

⑥ Center the corkscrew in the cork.

⑦ Keeping the corkscrew worm vertical, slowly turn the corkscrew clockwise so that the worm disappears into the cork.

⑧ Place the lever prongs on the bottle rim, holding it in place with the fingers.

⑨ Firmly holding the bottle and lever together, raise the opener handle until the cork comes out of the bottle.

⑩ When the cork is almost drawn, use your hand to gently pull it out. Check the wine's quality by smelling the cork.

⑪ Wipe the top of the bottle again with the service napkin.

⑫ Leave the bottle in the wine basket, label facing up, to pour the first taste for the host.

⑬ When the host has approved the wine, remove the bottle from the basket and hold it so that the label faces up.

Serve the other guests, moving counterclockwise around the table and serving from the right, completing the host's glass last. Pour the wine slowly, being careful not to touch the glass with the bottle. When you have finished pouring each glass, twist the wrist slightly with the neck of the bottle raised to avoid dripping. If there are drops left on the top of the bottle after pouring, wipe it dry with the service napkin.

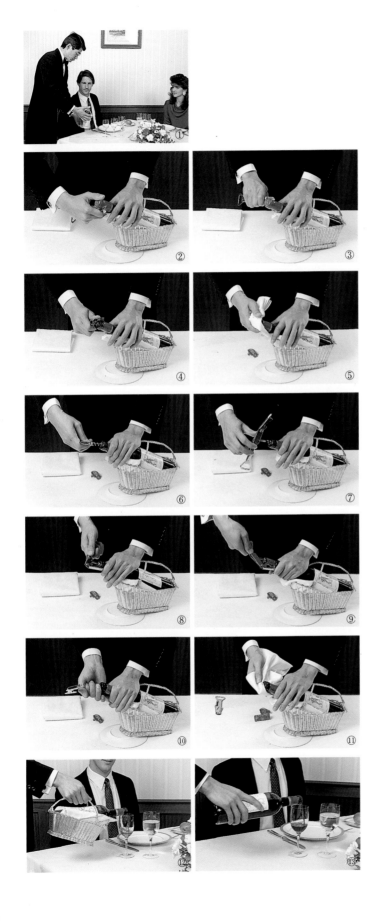

161

Decanting Red Wine

A long-matured old wine (high-quality vintage wine from Bordeaux or Burgundy) should be decanted—that is, the wine should be poured from the bottle into a carafe, leaving all the sediment in the bottle. During the maturation, impurities such as tannin and pigment from the wine are deposited on the bottom of the bottle. If these sediments are disturbed, the wine will be cloudy and the guest will feel a rough texture on the tongue when drinking it. Decanting allows the wine to be served free of any unnecessary sediment. However, there is a debate as to whether or not to decant wine. Some people believe that such high-quality wines may lose their superior bouquet upon rapid contact with air. Others believe that because decanting allows the wine to breathe out more bouquet by its contact with the air, even young red wines can be decanted. (Sometimes a wine is decanted for presentation purposes, but this should be done only when appropriate.)

The bottle of wine should be carried gently out of the wine cellar in a wine basket, and, after the guests have confirmed that it is the wine ordered, it should be decanted in front of them.

Utensils for decanting
① Bottle of wine in a wine basket
② Waiter's corkscrew
③ Candle
④ Carafe (decanter)

How to Decant (see photos to the right)

① If there is any sediment in the wine, strip off all the foil covering the neck of the bottle. If there is no sediment, draw the cork out and pour all the wine into a carafe (see pages 160–161).

② Hold the bottle of wine in your right hand and the carafe in your left. Keeping the neck of the bottle over the light of a candle, pour the wine gently so that it flows down along the inside of the carafe. Look carefully at the neck of the bottle against the light and stop pouring before the sediment reaches the neck of the bottle.

How to Open and Pour a Bottle of Champagne

The bottle of Champagne should be chilled in an ice bucket before serving. When uncorking the bottle, use your hand to prevent the cork from popping out suddenly. Follow this procedure for serving Champagne (see the photos below):

① Strip off the foil covering the wire cage.

② Carefully remove the wire cage.

③ Holding the bottle at an angle, wrap and wipe it with a service napkin. Twist the cork slowly in one direction with one hand while twisting the bottle in the opposite direction with the other hand.

④ Keeping your thumb on the cork, release it gently from the bottle without making any loud noise. A flute glass is most suitable for the serving of Champagne (see photo on page 43).

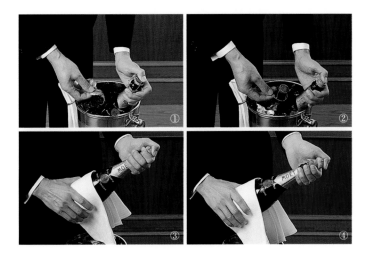

Wine Tasting

Looking at the Wine

To judge the clarity, color, depth of color, and viscosity of the wine, hold the glass by the base and look at it toward the light (see Photo ①). Use a white tablecloth on the table for background and slightly slant the glass (see Photo ②).

- Clarity—Wine should be clear, without any sediment.
- Color and depth of color—Each wine has its own characteristic color. As a wine ages, its color changes. Red wines lose color, and white wines gain color.
- Viscosity—If drops of wine with extended "legs" fall slowly down the inside of the glass after the wine is swirled, the wine has a high alcohol content and is full-bodied.

Judge the bubbles of properly chilled Champagne by their size (the smaller they are, the better the quality) and by their permanency (in fine champagne, the bubbles linger and rise to the surface without vanishing.)

Smelling the Wine

Swirl the glass so that the wine comes into contact with the air. Smell the volatile aroma that is derived from the grapes and the bouquet that is created from the development of the wine itself (see Photo ③). Judge the wine's "nose" (aroma and bouquet) by these three criteria:

- Intensity
- Quality—delicate, elegant, attractive
- Characteristics—flowery, grassy, earthy, nutty, etc.

Tasting the Wine

The taste of the wine can be judged at three stages: (1) when you initially put the wine in your mouth, (2) when you roll the wine in your mouth to release the flavor (see Photo ⑤), and (3) after you have swallowed the wine (the "finish"). During the second stage, the wine is kept in the mouth for a while to allow you to appreciate the entire flavor of the wine (sweetness, tannins, acidity, balance of various components of the wine, alcoholic content, body, etc.).

This chapter has provided an outline of the work of a *sommelier*. For further knowledge about wine itself, refer to a technical book on wine.

French–English Glossary

French Cooking Terms

A

aigre-doux: sweet and sour (*sauce aigre-doux*—sweet and sour sauce).

aiguillette: (1) slices of duck, wild birds, and also beef (*aiguillette de canard*—slices of duck meat); (2) the aitchbone of beef.

aile: wings of birds.

ailloli, aïoli: mayonnaise sauce made with egg yolk, olive oil, and crushed garlic.

à la: according to the style of (*à la française*—French style).

à la mode de: according to the style of (*tripes à la mode de Caen*—Caen-style tripes or braised tripes).

amer: bitter; (*chocolat amer*—bitter chocolate).

américaine (à l'): American style (*homard à l'américaine*—lobster *américaine*, or boiled lobster with spicy vegetables, tomatoes, and white wine.)

amuse-gueule, amuse-bouche: (1) cocktail snack; (2) bite-sized pie, canapé, and nuts, etc.

anglaise (à l'): English style (which means "vegetables boiled with salt" or "boiled meat").

apéritif: wine served as an appetizer before a meal.

à point: medium, as a stage of cooking meats.

appareil: mixture of different ingredients for preparation of a dish.

aspic: aspic (jelly) (*aspic de langouste*—lobster aspic).

assiette: (1) plate for one person; (2) the food dished on that plate (*assiette de fruits*—assorted fruits; *assiette anglaise*—assorted cold cuts).

au bleu: fish, especially freshwater fish, cooked in court bouillon, a mixture of water, wine, and vinegar (*truite au bleu*—trout *au bleu*).

au four: cooked in the oven, baked or roasted (*langoustine au four*—lobster cooked in the oven).

aumônière: a dish shaped like a money pouch (ingredients are wrapped in pastry or in a crêpe).

au naturel, nature: a dish cooked simply to make the most of the characteristics of the main ingredients (plain boiled vegetables, grilled meat or fish without sauce, fruits eaten without any sauce, etc.).

au sang: a duck or chicken dish the sauce of which is made with the animal's blood.

B

baba: a yeast-raised cake with raisins, flavored with rum or kirsch.

baguette: a long loaf of French bread.

ballotine: usually a boneless leg of poultry that is stuffed with forcemeat; when fish is used, a fillet is stuffed and rolled into a cone. Usually baked or braised and served hot.

banquet: dinner for many people.

bavaroise: Bavarian cream, a cold dessert made of egg yolk, milk, sugar, whipped cream, and gelatin. (This term can be used for some kinds of hors d'oeuvres.)

beignet: fritter (*beignets d'aubergines*—eggplant fritters; *beignets soufflés*—a fritter made of éclair paste or chou paste).

beurre: butter (*beurre blanc*—white butter sauce, a mixture of butter and boiled-down shallot and wine vinegar; *beurre fondu*—melted butter; *beurre manié*—a mixture of butter and flour that is used for thickening liquid; *beurre noir*—butter heated until it is dark brown and flavored with vinegar).

bien cuit: well done.

bifteck: beefsteak.

biscuit: cracker, or cookie (*biscuit roulé*—rolled cake; *biscuit à la cuillère*—lady fingers; *biscuit glacé*—a slice of layered ice cream made of several flavors).

bisque: creamy shellfish soup.

blanc: (1) white (*vin blanc*—white wine); (2) whitish part (*blanc de poireau*—white part of a leek; *blanc de poulet*—white meat of chicken).

blanc-manger: a pudding made with almond-flavored milk, gelatin and sugar according to the French style.

blanquette: a stew of white meat such as veal or chicken, simmered without browning, with white sauce.

bleu: rare.

bœuf (à la) mode: stewed beef.

bombe glacée: ice cream molded in a spherical shape.

bonne femme (à la): *bonne femme*–style (home-style cooking).

bouchée: (1) small meat patty or pastry shell filled with meat, poultry, or lobster; (2) petit four or bite-size chocolate.

bouillabaisse: shellfish soup of the Provence region whose main ingredients are shellfish, tomato, garlic, and saffron.

bouillon: simple, clear soup without added solid ingredients; broth.

bouquet garni: a combination of fresh herbs such as parsley, laurel, thyme, and celery, used for flavoring stock or stew.

bourguignon, à la bourguignonne: Burgundy-style; made with a Burgundy wine–flavored sauce and a garnish of pearl onions and mushrooms (*bœuf bourguignon*—beef stew flavored with Burgundy).

braisé: braised (*bœuf braisé*—braised beef).

brioche: a rich yeast dough, made with many eggs and much butter, that can be used for wrapping meat (*foie gras en brioche*—foie gras with brioche).

brochette: (1) skewer; (2) broiled food on a skewer (*brochette d'agneau*—broiled lamb on a skewer).

brun: brown (*roux brun*—brown roux).

brunoise: (1) to cut into $\frac{1}{8}$ inch (1 or 2 mm) dice. (see also *dé* and *macédoine*); (2) assorted vegetables cut into *brunoise*, which are ingredients for sauce or for adding to the sauce.

C

café: coffee (*café noir*—black coffee; *café express* or *express*—espresso).

canapé: a small, open-faced sandwich served as an hors d'oeuvre.

carré: square piece of veal, lamb, or pork meat cut so as to include back bones.

carte: menu, list (*carte des vins*—wine list). *à la carte*—according to a list in which each dish has its own separate price.

cassolette: (1) ramekin, small, shallow baking dish made of porcelain, heat-resistant glass, or metal; (2) the food dished onto the ramekin.

chariot: dessert cart.

charlotte: 1. a dessert made with cream and lined with lady fingers or *génois* cake; 2. a baked dessert made of a bread-lined mold filled with an apple mixture; 3. dish of vegetables or fish formed in the mold.

chartreuse: a steamed dish made of vegetables and meat.

chauteaubriand: double tenderloin steak broiled or sautéed and then sliced.

chaud: hot (*hors d'œuvre chaud*—hot hors d'oeuvre).

chaud-froid: cold, jellied sauce used to mask cold food platters for buffets (*chaud-froid de saumon*—cold, jellied salmon).

chausson: turnover (*chausson aux pommes*—apple turnover).

chevreuil: deer, venison (*en chevreuil*—meat cooked just like venison, that is, marinated in wine, cooked, and served with the sauce for game; *noisette d'agneau en chevreuil*—thick, round cutlet of lamb cooked like a venison dish).

choix: choice, selection (*choix de nos fromages*—our recommended cheese; *au choix*—of your choice).

chou: (1) cabbage; (2) chou or éclair paste.

choucroute: sauerkraut (pickled cabbage, a product of the Alsace region).

civet: (1) a stew made of game such as hare, venison, etc. (*civet de lièvre*—jugged hare); (2) poached shellfish, lobster, etc. or fish flavored with red wine.

clafouti(s): cherries baked in a pastry shell filled with custard.

clarifié: clarified, clear (*beurre clarifié*—clarified butter).

cocktail: (1) a mixed (alcoholic) drink; (2) hors d'oeuvre made of shrimp or crab seasoned with mayonnaise or ketchup; (3) fruits marinated in syrup flavored with alcohol.

cocotte: small, earthen cookware; *en cocotte*—to roast in a pot (*poulet en cocotte*—pot-roasted chicken; *œuf en cocotte*—soft-boiled egg with sauce).

cœur: (1) heart (*cœur de bœuf*—beef heart); (2) middle, core (*cœur de céleri*—celery heart).

compote: (1) compote of fruits (fruit cooked or stewed in sweetened water); (2) stewed meat (such as hare) and vegetables.

concassée de tomates: coarsely chopped, peeled and seeded tomatoes.

confiserie: preserving in sugar (such as in candy, caramel, nougat, fruit jelly;) as candied chestnuts, etc.).

confit: (1) preserved in syrup, alcohol, or vinegar (*fruits confits*—crystallized fruit); (2) goose, duck, or pork preserved in its own fat (*confit d'oie*—conserve of goose).

confiture: preserve, jam; *confiture d'abricot*—apricot jam).

consommé: a rich, flavorful stock or broth that is perfectly clear.

contre-filet, faux-filet: sirloin, hind brisket.

coq au vin: a French dish of chicken braised in wine, usually red wine.

corbeille: basket (*corbeille de fruits*—fruit basket).

côte: rib.

côtelette: loin chop, chop.

court-bouillon: water used to poach fish. It contains seasonings, herbs, and usually an acid such as vinegar.

crème: (1) cream (*crème au beurre*—butter cream; *crème Chantilly*—vanilla whipped cream; *crème ganache*—whipped cream with chocolate; *crème pâtissière*—vanilla custard cream; *crème renversée*—custard cream); (2) creamy soup (*crème d'asperges*—cream of asparagus soup).

crêpe: French pancake (*crêpes Suzette*—thin, rolled pancakes in an orange and butter sauce that is flambéd).

crepinette: a flat, oblong sausage or small portion of game or chicken mixture encased in pig's caul.

croissant: a buttery, breadlike pastry that is shaped like a crescent.

croquant: crisp (*salade croquante*—fresh salad prepared with the crisp leaves of vegetables).

croustade: bread or pie crust stuffed with meat or fish.

croûte: the outer thick crust of the pie crust or bread.

croûton: (1) thin slices of break that are cut, fried or toasted, and used for garnishing dishes; (2) aspic cut into several shapes for a cold dish.

cru: raw or uncooked (*jambon cru*—cured ham).

crudites: raw vegetables served as hors d'œuvres (cut and presented with sauce).

cuisse: thigh, leg, drumstick (*cuisse de poulet*—chicken leg; *cuisse de grenouille*—frog's leg).

D

darne: middle slice of a large fish (*darne de saumon*—slice of salmon).

daube: braised meat, poultry (sometimes this term is applied to braised fish and simmered vegetables).

dé: cut into dice (*dés de foie gras*—fat goose liver cut into dice. See also *brunoise* and *macédoine*).

dégustation: tasting (of wine or of food).

déjeuner: lunch (*petit déjeuner*—breakfast).

demi-bouteille: half bottle (of wine).

demi-glace, sauce demi-glace: thickened brown sauce prepared with brown roux, mixed herbs, tomatoes, brown stock, and madeira. (This sauce was the base for several types of brown sauce but now is often replaced by thickened veal stock.)

digestif: cordial or liqueur drunk after the meal.

dîner: dinner.

doux: sweet (*piment doux*—sweet pepper).

du jour: today's (*pâtisserie du jour*—today's pastry).

duxelles: mushrooms, onions, and shallots sautéed in butter, for use in vegetable and meat stuffings).

E

éclair: small cake made of pastry with cream inside and icing on top; (*éclair au chocolat*—chocolate éclair).

émincé: finely sliced (*émincé d'artichauts*—sliced artichokes).

entrecôte: sirloin steak cut from the middle part of the loin.

entrée: (1) main dish; (2) the first course of the meal, as hors d'œuvre or soup.

entremets: side dish, usually a sweet dish served between courses or an after-dinner dessert (such as cake, soufflé, or ice cream).

épaule: shoulder (*épaule de veau*—shoulder of veal).

escalope: thin round steak of meat or fish (*escalope de veau*—thin veal steak).

étuvée: braised (*étuvée de noix de Saint-Jacques*—braised scallop).

F

façon: style (*bouillabaisse à ma façon*—fish stew in "my" style; *à la façon de*—in the style of).

farce: mixture of hashed meat, fish, or shredded vegetables used for stuffing (forcemeat).

farci: (1) stuffed (*dindonneau farci aux marrons*—roasted young turkey stuffed with chestnuts); (2) stuffed food.

faux-filet: See *contre-filet*.

fermier: farmhouse style (homemade food rather than commercially made food); (*fromage fermier*—homemade cheese).

feuillantine: puff pastry that is stuffed or sometimes rolled with fruits or cream inside.

feuille: leaf (*feuilles d'épinard*—spinach leaves).

feuilletage, pâte feuilletée: puff paste.

feuilleté: flaky pastry that may be stuffed (*feuilleté aux ris de veau*—veal sweetbreads with pastry).

filet: (1) fillet, the undercut of a loin of beef, mutton, veal, pork, or game (*filet de bœuf*—undercut or fillet of beef; *filet mignon*—small, tender fillet from beef, pork, lamb, or veal tenderloins); (2) delicacy of poultry or game; (3) deboned fish.

fines herbes: chopped herbs (chopped parsley, chervil, tarragon, etc., mixed together).

flan: (1) a kind of tart; (2) a kind of custard.

fleur: flower (*courgette à la fleur*—courgette with flower).

fleuron: little half-moon shape of baked puff paste used for garnishing.

fond: (1) bottom, base (*fond d'artichaut*—artichoke bottom); (2) soup stock (*fond de veau*—veal stock).

fondue: (1) melted cheese and white wine into which you dip pieces of bread (specialty of the Alsace region); (2) oil fondue (speciality of the Burgundy region); (3) braised vegetables (*fondue de tomate*—braised tomatoes).

fourré: stuffed (*pigeon fourré aux épinards*—roast pigeon stuffed with spinach).

frais: (1) fresh, cool; (2) fresh, cured (*nouilles fraîches*—fresh handmade noodles; *thym frais*—fresh thyme; *fromage frais*—fresh cheese or cream cheese).

friandise, mignardise: small, sweet, fancy cakes, bite-size chocolates, and bonbons.

fricassée: a dish made of pieces of poultry, veal, lamb, or shellfish, cooked and served in a thick white sauce.

frit: fried (*pommes frites*—fried potatoes).

friture: deep-fried food, especially applied to small, deep-fried fish.

froid: cold (*hors d'œuvres froids*—cold hors d'oeuvres).

fromage: (1) cheese; (2) a boiled and pressed piece of meat in a pot with jelly (*fromage de tête*—brown, potted head with jelly, seasoned with herbs).

fumet: soup stock of fish, game, or any highly flavored substance used as the main ingredient of a sauce (*fumet de poisson*—fish stock; *fumet de truffe*—boiled-down truffle juice flavored with madeira.

G

galantine: a dish made of meat, poultry, or fish cut into small pieces and stuffed with minced meat (it is usually poached and served cold).

galette: (1) pie or cookies shaped round and flat (*galette des Rois*—king's *galette*, an almond cream pie with small ceramic dolls inside, prepared on the occasion of the Epiphany); (2) potato garnish prepared with thin slices of potato and baked as a flat, round cake.

garniture: (1) garnish; (2) the act of garnishing.

gâteau: cake (*gâteau au chocolat*—chocolate cake; *gâteau de champignons*—soft mushroom cake).

gelée: (1) cooking jelly, a mixture of meat or fish stock and gelatin (*œuf poché en gelée*—boiled egg in jelly); (2) sweet jelly; (3) preserves or jam.

génoise: French sponge cake.

gigot: leg of mutton or lamb.

glace: (1) ice; (2) ice cream (*glace à la vanille*—vanilla ice cream); (3) glaze (boiled-down meat stock used for finishing sauce).

glacé: (1) cold, chilled, iced (*consommé glacé*—chilled clear soup); (2) covered with glaze or icing (*carottes glacées*—glazed carrots; *petits fours glacés*—small finger-sized cakes covered with icing).

goujonnette: fillets of sole sliced diagonally and fried.

gourmandise: (1) gluttony; (2) sweets, good things to eat (sometimes applied to the *petit fours* served after the meal).

grand veneur: master of the Royal hunt–style, includes dishes made of game such as venison that are served with creamed pepper and black-currant jam sauce and garnished with chestnut purée (*selle de chevreuil grand veneur*—saddle of venison *grand veneur*–style).

granité: coarse, crystalline sherbet.

gratin, au gratin: sprinkled with buttered crumbs and baked brown (*poireaux au gratin*—leeks au gratin).

gratiné: prepared gratin style, baked until encrusted or until the surface is browned (*soupe à l'oignon gratinée*—onion gratin soup).

grillade: grilled meat, especially beef.

grillé: grilled (*côtes de veau grillée*—grilled rib of veal).

gros sel: coarse salt (*au gros sel*—seasoned with coarse salt, sometimes applied to roast chicken covered over with coarse salt.)

H

hors d'œuvre: hors d'oeuvre (several types of food served at the beginning of the meal).

hure: (1) pork head or wild boar head (sometimes applied to salmon or pike head); (2) dishes prepared with a pork or wild boar head.

I

infusion: liquid obtained from steeping a food, spice, flower, or plant (such as herb tea).

J

jardinière: a mixture of fresh garden vegetables such as carrots, peas, turnips, etc.

jeune: young (*jeunes poireaux*—young leeks).

julienne: cut into fine shreds (*julienne de légumes*—mixed vegetables cut into very fine shreds; *consommé julienne*—clear vegetable soup with onions or leeks, carrots and celery).

jus: (1) vegetable or fruit juice (*jus de citron*—lemon juice); (2) natural juice from meat; (3) meat stock (*jus de veau* or *fond de veau*—veal stock).

L

langue: tongue (*langue de bœuf*—beef tongue).

léger: light (*sauce légère*—light, tasty sauce).

lié: thickened (*fond de veau lié*—thickened veal stock).

M

macaron: macaroon (small cake made mostly of ground almonds, sugar, and egg).

macédoine: (1) vegetables or fruits cut in the *macédoine* style of cutting, that is, into $\frac{1}{4}$ inch (3 to 4 mm) dice (see also *brunoise* and *dé*; (2) diced vegetables seasoned with butter or mayonnaise sauce (also applied to fruit cocktail).

madeleine: French sponge cakes that are shaped like a small shell.

maison: homemade, specially made (*pâtisseries maison*—specially made cakes).

matelote: rich, brown, freshwater fish stew with wine, made with freshwater fish like eel (*matelote d'anguille*—brown eel stew).

matignon: mixture of finely cut herbs and chopped ham sautéed in butter, used for stuffing braised meat or fish.

mayonnaise: mayonnaise sauce.

médaillon: oval slice of meat or fish (*médaillon de foie gras*—goose liver sliced in an oval shape).

menu: (1) menu; (2) a set meal (*menu dégustation*—special set meal for those who are interested in tasting several small dishes).

meringue: mixture made of sugar and egg whites beaten together; baked meringue.

meunière (à la): *meunière* (miller's wife) style cooking, food covered with seasoned flour and sautéed in butter (*sole meunière*—fried sole *meunière*-style).

meurette: brown stew prepared with red Burgundy wine, fresh-water fish, and sometimes fish eggs from the Burgundy region. The liquid may be thickened (this thicker sauce is called *Bourguignonne*) and bacon may be added (*œufs en meurette*—poached egg with *Bourguignonne* sauce).

mignardises: See *friandise*.

mignonnette: tiny; (1) coarsely ground pepper; (2) round cut of white meat of lamb or poultry.

millefeuille: French sweet puff pastry with several layers (sometimes used to refer to the dessert rolled with puff pastry).

minute: (1) minute steak (*minute de saumon*—salmon minute steak); (2) *à la minute* means cooking very quickly (*sauté d'agneau à la minute*—sautéed lamb, minute style).

mirepoix: garnish of diced, sautéed carrots, celery, onions, herbs, and spices; used for braised meat and in stocks and sauces.

mousse: a frozen dessert of beaten fresh cream, beaten egg whites, and fruit purée or other flavoring. This term can also mean a soufflé-type side dish made with these ingredients and ground fish, chopped meat, or vegetable purée (*mousse de homard*—lobster soufflé; *mousse glacée*—light, tasty ice cream).

mousseline: (1) small quantity of mousse or light mousse; (2) light dish made of mousse (*sauce mousseline*—light, tasty mousse sauce prepared with hollandaise or mayonnaise and fresh cream).

N

nage: court-bouillon (*à la nage*—boiled and served in court-bouillon; *coquilles Saint-Jacques à la nage*—boiled scallops in court bouillon).

navarin: mutton stew with various vegetables.

noir: black (*olives noires*—black olives).

noisette: (1) thick, round cut of lamb, veal, or venison fillet; (2) hazelnut.

noix: (1) walnut; (2) juicy cutlet of leg of veal (not too fatty, but soft meat); (3) adductor muscle of shellfish (*noix de coquille Saint-Jacques*—adductor part of scallop).

nouilles: noodles, pasta.

nouveau: new (*oignon nouveau*—new onion, onion of the best season).

O

œuf: an egg or a dish or dessert made of egg (*oeuf a la coque*—boiled egg; *oeufs brouilés*—scrambled eggs *œuf dur*—hard-boiled egg; *œuf poché*–poached egg; *œuf sur le plat*—fried egg; *œuf à la neige*—chilled dessert prepared with meringue and custard cream).

omelette: (1) omelet (*omelette nature*—plain omelet); (2) omelet-style dessert (*omelette soufflée*—soft, sweet omelet; *omelette norvégienne*—Norwegian-style (surprise) omelet, a cheese gratin dessert made with layers of sponge cake and ice cream.

P

pain: (1) bread (*pain de mie* = sandwich or loaf of bread; (2) soft loaf prepared with mainly ground meat or fish and purée of vegetables, eggs, and fresh cream (*pain de foie gras*—soft liver loaf).

panaché: multicolored by using various ingredients (*glace panachée*—mixed ice cream; *panaché de* *poissons*—large dish prepared with several kinds of fish).

papillote, en papillote: wrapped in paper or foil for cooking food, so the food is steamed in its own moisture.

parfait, parfait glacé: parfait ice cream.

pâte: (1) paste, butter (*pâte à gênoise*—batter for sponge cake; *pâte levée*—batter for puff pastry; *pâte brisée*—short crust paste); (2) pasta, noodle.

pâté: 1. pâté (*pâté encroute*—meat or fish pie).

pâtisserie: general term for several types of pastry (cakes, pies, cookies, etc).

paupiette: stuffed, rolled, thin slices of braised meat, fish or poultry (*paupiette de bœuf braisée*—roll of braised beef).

paysanne: vegetables cut into regular square shapes (*à la paysanne*—dish prepared with sautéed diced vegetables; *potage à la paysanne*—vegetable soup).

pêcheur: fisherman's style (*du (des) pêcheur(s)*—dish prepared with fish or shellfish; *salade des pêcheurs*—fisherman's seafood salad).

persillé: sprinkled with herbs such as parsley (*jambon persillé*)—jellied ham with chopped parsley; *carré d'agneau persillé*—roasted loin of lamb sprinkled with chopped parsley and sliced garlic).

petit: small, tiny (*petit oignon*—small onion).

petite marmite: a kind of boiled meat and vegetable stew served in a small stew pot.

petit four: a small cake or cookie (*petits fours secs*—small cookies or biscuits).

pilaf, pilaw: pilaf.

pithiviers: almond cream pie.

plat: (1) plate, pot used for cooking; (2) serving plate; (3) dish meal (*plat du jour*—today's recommended dish).

plateau: tray, dish of assorted foods (*plateau de fruits de mer*—large dish of assorted seafood).

poché: poached (*saumon poché*—poached salmon).

poêlé: braised (*canard poêlé*—braised duck).

pointe: point, tip, head (*pointes d'asperges*—asparagus tips).

poitrine: chest, breast (*poitrine de porc*—breast of pork).

pot: pot (*pot de crème*—custard baked in a small pot).

potage: soup.

pot-au-feu: a standard French dish of boiled meat with vegetables in soup.

pouding, poudding: a pudding or steamed dessert prepared mainly with milk, egg, etc. (*poudding au riz*—rice pudding).

primeurs: early-in-the-season vegetables and fruits.

printanier, à la printanière: printanier style, dishes prepared or garnished with fresh spring vegetables (*navarin printanier*—stew of mutton or lamb with spring vegetables).

profiterole: small puff pastry filled with cream, ice cream, or savory hors d'oeuvre fillings. Profiterole without stuffing may be the garnish for soup (*profiteroles au chocolat*—stuffed profiterole covered with chocolate).

Q

quenelle: dumpling.

queue: (1) tail (*queue de bœuf*—cow's tail); (2) body of prawn or shrimp (*queues d'écrevisse*—crayfish body).

quiche: a kind of tart (specialty of the Lorraine region).

R

râble: saddle of hare.

râgout: thick, savory stew prepared with meat or fish and vegetables.

ratatouille: mixture of fried eggplant, tomatoes, zucchini, and garlic (specialty of southern parts of France).

ravioli: small squares or rounds of stuffed Italian pasta.

rillettes: ground duck or hare meat potted in its own fat, served as an hors d'oeuvre.

rosbif: roast beef.

rosé: rosy, rose-pink, rosé wine.

rôti: roasted (*poulet rôti*—roast chicken).

rouge: red (*fruit rouge*—red fruit).

roulade: rolled, stuffed dish.

roux: a preparation of butter and flour used for thickening sauces.

royale (à la): royal style, which means dishes with egg custard (to which vegetable purée may be added) that is cut into small pieces as a garnish (*consommé royale*—clear soup with royal-style garnish).

S

sabayon: (1) creamy dessert or dessert sauce prepared with egg yolk, vanilla, sugar, and white wine; (2) a kind of sauce for fish prepared with egg yolk, fresh cream, and white wine or Champagne.

saignant: rare, underdone, lightly cooked.

saint-honoré: round puff pastry filled with custard cream and covered with caramel.

saison: season (*salade de saison*—seasonal salad).

salmis: a type of sauce made from partially roasted game.

salpicon: sauce with meat, fish, vegetables, or fruits cut into small cubes and used for stuffing or as a garnish.

sauce: (*sauce américaine*—sauce prepared with lobster, tomatoes, bouquet of herbs, and white wine; *sauce béchamel*—béchamel sauce or white cream sauce; *sauce hollandaise*—hollandaise sauce, traditional sauce originally from the Netherlands prepared with whipped egg yolk and clarified butter; *sauce vinaigrette*—French dressing).

sauté: sautéed, sautéed food (*filet de bœuf sauté*—sautéed (fillet of) beef; *sauté d'agneau*—sauté of lamb).

sauvage: wild (*canard sauvage*—wild duck).

savarin: light, spongy yeast cake baked in a tube pan and soaked in rum, sugar syrup, or a liqueur-flavored syrup, decorated with whipped cream and served with fruits in the center.

sec: dry (*vin blanc sec*—dry white wine).

selle: saddle of mutton, lamb, or venison.

sirop: syrup.

sorbet: sherbet, sorbet (*sorbet à la pêche*—peach sherbet).

soufflé: (1) baked or steamed light pudding that may be sweetened or unsweetened; (2) shaped like a soufflé (*soufflé glacé*—ice cream shaped like a soufflé).

spécialité: specialty or particularly fine product of a region.

succès: two very thin almond meringues sandwiched together with praline-flavored buttercream.

suprême: (1) light part of chicken or game bird; (2) fillet of sole.

surprise (*en*): dish with a surprising garnish or combination of ingredients (*truffe en surprise*—surprising truffle).

T

tarte: pie, tart (*tarte aux pommes*—apple pie, apple tart).

tartelette: small pie, tart.

terrine: potted meat, pâté (*terrine de poisson*—fish pâté).

tête: head (*tête de veau*—veal's head).

tiède: lukewarm, warm, mild (*salade tiède*—warm salad).

timbale: (1) a mold for baking; (2) a small baked pie crust shaped like a kettle-drum and filled with meat, poultry, cheese, or dessert (*timbale Elysée*—Elysée-style pastry, that is, cake stuffed with ice cream and fruits.

tournedos: small slices from the heart of the fillet of beef.

tranche: slice (*tranche de loup*—slice of sea perch).

tronçon: piece, portion (*tronçons d'anguilles*—portions of eel).

vacherin: meringue shells customarily filled with ice cream, chestnut puree, flavored whipped cream, and the like.

vapeur: steam (*saint-pierre à la vapeur*—steamed John Dory [a kind of sea bream]).

varié: miscellaneous, diversified, with variety (*salade variée*—variety salad).

velouté: (1) creamy sauce made with white stock with roux; (2) thick cream soup.

vert: green (*salade verte*—green salad).

vessie: bladder (*en vessie*—boiled food, especially meat or chicken in bouillon, wrapped in bladder).

vichyssoise: chilled puree of leek and potato soup with cream.

vinaigrette: see *sauce vinaigrette*.

vol-au-vent: round or oval case made of puff pastry, filled with râgout of meat or fish and usually covered with a crust lid.

Ingredients Used in French Cooking

A

abats: offal

abricot: apricot

agneau: lamb

ail: garlic

airelle (*rouge*), *canneberg*: cranberry

amande: almond

ananas: pineapple

anchois: anchovy

anet (*h*), *fenouil bâtard*: dill

anguille: eel

anis: anise, aniseed

artichaut: artichoke

asperge: asparagus

aubergine: eggplant, aubergine

avocat: avocado (pear)

B

banane: banana

bar, loup (*de mer*): sea perch

barbue: brill

basilic: basil

baudroie, lot (*t*)*e de mer*: angler (fish), monkfish

betterave: beets

beurre: butter

bière: beer

bœuf: beef

boudin (*noir*): black pudding, blood sausage

brochet: pike

brocoli: broccoli

C

cabillau (*d*): codfish, fresh cod

caille: quail

calmar, calamar, encornet: squid

calvados: apple brandy

canard: duck

caneton: duckling

cannelle: cinnamon

câpre: caper

cari, carry: curry

carotte: carrot

carpe: carp

carrelet, plie: plaice

cassis, groseille noire: black currant

céleri: celery

céleri-rave: celeriac

cèpe: cep, boletus (mushroom)

cerfeuil: chervil

cerise: cherry

cervelle: brains

champignon: mushroom

chanterelle, girolle: chanterelle (mushroom)

chapon: capon

chevreuil: venison

chicorée (*frisée*): chicory

chocolat: chocolate

chou: cabbage

chou de Bruxelles: Brussels sprout

chou-fleur: cauliflower

chou-rave: kohlrabi

chou de Milan: Savoy cabbage

chou rouge: red cabbage

ciboulette: chive(s)

cidre: cider

citron: lemon

citron vert, lime: lime

cochon de lait: suckling pig

coco: coconut

cœur: heart

colin, merlu: hake

concombre: cucumber

congre, anguille de mer: conger eel

coq: cock, rooster

coquillage: shellfish
coquille Saint-Jacques: scallop
coriandre: coriander
cornichon: gherkin
courge: pumpkin, squash
courgette: courgette, zucchini
crème (*fraîche*): (fresh) cream
crème aigre: sour cream
crépine: caul
cresson: watercress, cress
crevette: shrimp, prawn
crustacés: shellfish, crustacean

D

daurade, dorade: sea bream, gilthead
dinde: turkey (-hen)
dindon: turkey (-cock)

E

eau: water
eau-de-vie: brandy
échalote: shallot, scallion
écrevisse: (freshwater) crayfish, crawfish
encornet: see *calmar*
endive: chicory, witloof, (Belgian) endive
épice: spice
épinard: spinach
escargot: (edible) snail
estragon: tarragon

F

faisan: pheasant, cock-pheasant
farine: flour
fécule: starch
fenouil: fennel
fève: broad bean, fava bean
figue: fig
foie: liver

foie gras: foie gras
fraise: strawberry
fraise des bois: wild strawberry
framboise: raspberry
fromage: cheese
fruit de la Passion: passion fruit
fruits de mer: mixed shellfish

G

garenne, lapin de garenne: game rabbit
gélatine: gelatin(e)
genièvre: juniper berry
gésier: gizzard
gibier: game
gingembre: ginger
girofle, clou de girofle: clove
girolle: see *chanterelle*
gombo, okra: gombo, okra
goujon: gougeon
graine: grain
gras-double: tripe
grenade: pomegranate
grenouille: frog
groseille verte (à *maquereau*): gooseberry
groseille rouge: red currant

H

hareng: herring
haricot blanc: white haricot bean, white kidney bean
haricot vert: French bean
herbes (*aromatiques*): (aromatic) herbs
homard: lobster
huile: oil
huître: oyster

J

jambon: ham
jamboncru: (raw) cured ham

K

kaki: persimmon

L

lait: milk

laitue: lettuce

laitue romaine, chicon: cos lettuce, romaine lettuce

langouste: sea crayfish

langoustine: Norway lobster, Dublin bay prawn, scampi

langue: tongue

lapereau: young rabbit

lapin: rabbit

lard gras, gros lard: bacon fat

lard maigre, petit lard, lard de poitrine: streaky bacon, lean bacon

lard (maigre) fumé: bacon

(feuille de) laurier: bayleaf

légume: vegetable

lentille: lentil

lièvre: hare

liqueur: liquor

lot(t)e de mer: see *baudroie*

lot(t) (de rivière):   burbot

loup (de mer):   see *bar*

M

mâche: corn salad

macis: mace

madère: Madeira (wine)

maïs: sweet corn, Indian corn, maize corn

mandarine: mandarin, tangerine

mangue: mango

maquereau: mackerel

marasquin: maraschino

marc: marc (brandy)

marcassin: young wild boar

marjolaine: (sweet) marjoram

marron: chestnut

menthe: mint

merlan: whiting

merlu: see *colin*

mesclun: mixed salad vegetable

miel: honey

mirabelle: small golden yellow plum, mirabell plum

moelle: marrow (bone)

morille: morel

moreu: salt cod, cod

moule: mussel

moutarde: mustard

mouton: mutton

mûre sauvage, mûre de ronce: blackberry, bramble

muscade, noix (de) muscade: nutmeg

(airelle) myrtille: bilberry, blueberry, huckleberry, whortleberry

N

navet: turnip

nectarine, brugnon: nectarine

noisette: hazel nut, filbert

noix: walnut, filbert

noix de coco: see *coco*

O

œuf: egg

oie: goose

oignon: onion

omble, omble chevalier: char

oreille de mer: abalone

oseille: sorrel

oursin: sea urchin, sea hedgehog

P

pain: bread

palourde clovisse: clam, venus

pamplemousse: grapefruit

papaye: papaya, papaw

pastèque, melon d'eau: watermelon

(graine de) pavot: poppy (seed)

pêche: peach

perdreau: young partridge

persil: parsley

petits pois: (garden) peas, green peas

pied: foot, trotter

pigeonneau: young pigeon

pignon: pigon, pine nut, pine seed

piment (poivre) de la Jamïque, toute-èpice:
allspice, Jamaica pepper, pimento

piment doux, poivron: sweet pepper, pimento

pintade: guinea fowl

pistache: pistachio (nut)

pleurote: pleurotus, oyster mushroom

poire: pear

poireau: leek

pois: pea

pois chiche: chickpea

(pois) mange-tout, pois gourmand: snow pea

poisson: fish

(grain de) poivre: pepper(corn)

poivre de Cayenne, cayenne: cayenne pepper

poivron: see *piment doux*

pomme: apple

pomme de terre: potato

porc: pork

porto: port (wine)

potiron: pumpkin

poularde: poularde, fattened pullet

poulet: chicken

poulpe: octopus

poussin: spring chicken

praire: venus (clam)

prune: plum

pruneau: prune

Q

queue: tail

R

radis: radish

raie: ray, skate

raifort: horseradish

raisin: grape

raisin sec: raisin, currant

rascasse: scorpion fish, hogfish

rhum: rum

ris: sweetbread

riz: rice

riz sauvage: wild rice

rognon: kidney

romarin: rosemary

rouget (-barbet): red mullet, goatfish

S

Safran: saffron

saindoux: lard

saint-pierre: John Dory

salade: salad, salad vegetable

salsifis: salsify, oyster plant

sanglier: wild boar

sardine: sardine, young pilchard

sarrasin: buckwheat

sarriette: savory

saucisse, saucisson: sausage

sauge: sage

saumon: salmon

seiche: cuttlefish

seigle: rye

sel: salt

sésame: sesame

sucre: sugar

sucre en poudre (semoule): caster (castor) sugar, (fine) granulated sugar

sucre glace: icing sugar

T

tête: head

thé: tea

thon: tunny, tuna

thym: thyme

tomate: tomato

trévise, chicorée de Trévise: red chicory

tripe(s): tripe

truffe: truffle

truite: trout

truite arc-en-ciel: rainbow trout

truite saumonée, truite de mer: salmon trout, sea trout

turbot: turbot

turbotin: young turbot

V

(gousse de) vanille: vanilla (bean)

veau: veal

vermout(h): vermouth

vessie: bladder

viande: meat

vin: wine

vin mousseux: sparkling wine

vinaigre: vinegar

vinaigre de vin: wine vinegar

volaille: poultry

X

xérès: sherry

Y

yaourt, yog(h)ourt: yogurt